THE GOD-
FIRST LIFE

THE GOD-FIRST LIFE

UNCOMPLICATE YOUR LIFE, GOD'S WAY

STOVALL WEEMS

ZONDERVAN

The God-First Life
Copyright © 2014 by Stovall Weems

This title is also available as a Zondervan ebook.
Visit www.zondervan.com/ebooks.

Requests for information should be addressed to:
Zondervan, *Grand Rapids, Michigan 49530*

Library of Congress Cataloging-in-Publication Data

Weems, Stovall.
    The God-first life : set the right priorities and unlock the secret to blessing
and freedom / Stovall Weems. — First edition.
        pages cm
    Includes bibliographical references and index.
    ISBN 978-0-310-32009-8 (softcover)
    1. Christian life. I. Title.
    BV4501.3.W4155 2014
    248.4 — dc23   2013039133

Published in association with the literary agency of Fedd & Company, Inc., Post Office
Box 341973, Austin, Texas 78734

Cover design: Studio Gearbox
Interior design: Matthew Van Zomeren

Printed in the United States of America

14 15 16 17 18 19 20 21 22 /DCI/ 21 20 19 18 17 16 15 14 13 12 11 10 9 8 7 6 5 4 3 2 1

CONTENTS

FOREWORD

My favorite thing in the world is introducing people to my favorite person in the world—Jesus. The apostle Paul once said that practically all he could do was talk about Jesus and what he did for us. I get it. For me Jesus is everything too.

Why? There are so many reasons, but one is this: Jesus shows us a new and better way to be human. We're so used to thinking of our shortcomings and our hang-ups as coming from who we are. It's human nature, right? Not with Jesus. He changed all that for us. Jesus has given us a new nature—a new life.

In this book, *The God-First Life*, my friend Pastor Stovall Weems shows what that new life can look like. The way Stovall breaks it down, it's not about a bunch of dos and don'ts. It's about making some simple but powerful decisions, and it all starts with the decision to put God first.

When Stovall met Jesus, he knew life would be forever better. But how exactly? Tell me if you know something I don't, but it's not like loving Jesus means all your problems go away. And Stovall faced the same confusing issues most of us do.

Life, love, faith, work, whatever—how are we supposed to manage this new life in the middle of all the day-to-day challenges we have?

Jesus gave the answer. It's right there in the gospel of Matthew, but while Stovall was feeling his way through a thick cloud of questions, the Holy Spirit used this verse to blow all the fog away: "Seek first his kingdom and his righteousness, and all these things will be given to you as well" (Matthew 6:33). In other words, put God first, and the rest will become clear. God will sort it out. That insight opened up a whole new path for Stovall—and it can for all of us.

Most of our problems come from disorder. We put our wants, our plans, our desires first. And then—no surprise—it all blows up in our face. Jesus doesn't want that any more than we do.

Instead, Stovall shows us how to restore order to our lives and release the blessing that Jesus has in mind for all of us.

Judah Smith
Pastor, The City Church
Author, *Jesus Is: Find a New Way to be Human*

PART 1

NEW PRIORITY

Seek first his kingdom and his righteousness,
and all these things will be given to you as well.

Matthew 6:33

YOUR LIFE, GOD'S WAY
An Invitation to Seek God's Kingdom First

> Trust in the LORD with all your heart
>> and lean not on your own understanding;
> in all your ways submit to him,
>> and he will make your paths straight.
>>> *Proverbs 3:5–6*

Years ago, my church—Celebration Church in Jacksonville, Florida—rented a billboard near a busy highway. We were looking to attract people to what God was doing in our world. The ad featured an image of me (which made sense because the invitation was coming from the church, and well, I'm the pastor) with these words emblazoned across the ad:

Your Life, God's Way

Despite the blinding vibrancy of my lime green golf shirt, we got a great response to that billboard. Lots of people visited Celebration for the first time and made it their home. Why? I seriously doubt it was due to my friendly-yet-penetrating gaze as drivers made their daily commute to work each day. No. What drew people in was that the ad offered a different approach to the one thing everyone is concerned about and probably mulling over on their way to work: *my life*. Imagine the thoughts of those drivers. It's not hard because we've all had them at one time or another, maybe at this very moment:

My life is a mess.
My life is going great.
My life doesn't matter.
My life is about to change.
My life is falling apart.
My life has no purpose.
My life is too busy.
My life is depressing.
My life is over-the-top amazing.

The billboard reached all these people behind the wheel—all with different plans, experiences, hopes, disappointments, and so on—and offered them one more lens through which to view their life: *God's way.*

Adding these two words has a way of changing our perspective. It forces us to pause and consider that there may be a completely different way of doing life than we are currently doing it, one we may never have considered. I'm sure more than one person drove by that billboard and thought, *"God's way,"* huh? *What does that look like? It's gotta be better than the way I'm doing it.*

FACING THE BIG QUESTIONS

When I was growing up, my family occasionally went to church, but God wasn't really a big part of our lives. We were definitely Christian in our beliefs, but as a young person, my focus was on doing what a lot of young people do—partying and having a good time. I believed God existed, but I didn't think there was much more to faith in God than that.

About midway through college, however, something changed. I had an aunt who was praying for me, and God was really drawing me to him. I found myself tired of the typical college party lifestyle. The things I was involved in began to feel very temporal. Partying, studying, working, partying—I knew there had to be more than this, and I began actively seeking.

I was at a secular university, but I chose to major in religious studies. If Jesus was the truth, I wanted to know. I personally believe that's what goes on in every human being. There are seasons when God draws us to the truth. Like Paul talks about in Romans 2, I had suppressed that truth before; this time, I responded to it. Right there in the middle of the college party scene, I surrendered my life to Christ.

I found the experience, presence, and forgiveness of Jesus amazing, and I wanted to follow him with everything I had. But it wasn't easy. At the time I invited Christ into my life, I was part of the roughest fraternity on campus and worked in a bar. Not recommended. It was a confusing place and time. As I moved forward in my newfound faith, I faced tougher questions, harder choices, and stronger temptations than I knew what to do with.

I was reading the Bible, and sometimes it spoke directly to me and provided exactly the answer I needed. But other times the Bible seemed totally unrelated to the things I was dealing with. For every one thing I understood about God or the world, there were about ten others that seemed confusing, even unfair. How was I now supposed to approach these tough situations:

What is God's plan for my future?

Do I need to ask for forgiveness every time I sin?

How can I better relate to people who believe differently than I do?

Is the girl I'm dating "Christian enough" to marry?

How can I trust God when modern science seems to contradict the Bible?

Why does God tolerate so much evil in the world?

What about all the people who believe in other religions? Are they all wrong?

Is Jesus really the only way to heaven?

Are all my friends and family members who don't know
Christ really going to this place the Bible calls hell?
If hell is real, what is it like?

And that was just the start. Wrestling with all these questions—and having few answers—made my walk with Christ
inconsistent at first. I prayed, went to church, and studied
Scripture, but a lot of stuff just wasn't connecting. I held on,
though, because I knew I had met Jesus and something signifi-
cant had changed in my life. Since he promised to help me, I
kept on seeking him.

One day I was walking to class, considering all the questions racing through my head, and God brought to mind
something I'd read in the Gospels, Matthew 6:33: "Seek first
his kingdom and his righteousness, and all these things will be
given to you as well." This was the turning point. God spoke
powerfully to me in that moment. *Seek me above all else*, he
said. *Put me first.*

If I would truly put God first—regardless of how I felt or
whether I completely understood it—then he would take care
of "all these things." I didn't do it perfectly. I didn't have it all
figured out. But that verse changed everything for me. My
faith started moving from my head down deep into my heart.
From then on, Matthew 6:33 became my compass. It seemed so
simple, so tangible. There were a lot of things I couldn't do—
or didn't even know to do. But I could do that.

THREE GAME CHANGERS

When I first started thinking about my life in terms of God's
way, three life-altering, game-changing realizations came to
mind. And speaking now as a pastor, let me add that these apply
to anyone.

1. *God has a "way" for our lives.* Most people think God is not
at all interested in the details of our lives. But he is. He doesn't

sit in heaven simply watching our lives from the nosebleeds. God wants to be fully involved in your life, and he has a game plan, a path, a way for your life that is designed specifically for you.[1] As you make him the first priority in your life, you'll witness firsthand just how much God wants to be present and active in your life. You will experience his presence on a whole new level.

2. *We don't have to carry the weight of our life alone.* Life is challenging, and the cares of life are heavy, but God doesn't want you to carry the burden alone. Jesus invites you to keep step with him while he does the heavy lifting.[2] When you put God first, you begin to live in response to him as he shapes your life. Rather than striving to manipulate and control every outcome under your own strength, you will find that God is standing close, ready to help lighten the load.

3. *God's way is better than ours.* The Bible says that God's way is perfect, refreshing, trustworthy, right, and enlightening.[3] I don't know about you, but my way usually isn't any of those things. Amazingly, God's way is not only all those things, but it also meets us wherever we are. When you feel like your life . . .

is a mess, God works all things out for your good.[4]

is going great, God has greater things in store for you.[5]

doesn't matter, God ascribes incredible value to you.[6]

is about to change, he will be with you every step of the way.[7]

is falling apart, God is your strength and deliverer.[8]

has no purpose, God's purpose for you will prevail.[9]

is too busy, God's peace guards your heart and mind.[10]

is depressing, he is the giver of joy.[11]

is over-the-top amazing, there is a place to direct your gratitude.[12]

God's way for your life *is* the best possible way you can live. I think most people instinctively believe this, but few know how to put that belief into action. It's really not as complicated as we can sometimes make it appear to be.

KEEPING IT SIMPLE

The things we enjoy most are often complex things made simple. In an interview with *Newsweek*, Steve Jobs said the desire for simplicity played a key role in the development of the iPod—and presumably all the other "iStuff" we love to use.

"When you first start off trying to solve a problem, the first solutions you come up with are very complex, and most people stop there," he told interviewer Steven Levy. "But if you keep going, and live with the problem and peel more layers of the onion off, you can often times arrive at some very elegant and simple solutions."[13]

Under an iPhone's touch screen, we find layers of complexity that most of us will never understand. But the simplicity of the interface and the way it integrates with all the apps, functions, and tools make it appealing to millions. We don't love the iPhone for its complexity; we love it for the way it makes all the complexity so simple that a toddler can use it. What if your life could be like that too?

But life is just not that simple.

I hear that all the time. I've even said it myself. The phrase is usually followed by a long account of a real and complicated situation that the person has struggled with for a long time. I understand. I really do. But let me be clear on something: while many of the problems we face in life are complex, I don't believe that the ultimate solution is.

Our lives really can be simple. In fact, I believe they were always meant to be. Unfortunately, few people understand how to live such a straightforward life in the middle of this hectic, complex, and painful world. I want to turn that around. When I discovered the practice of putting God first, everything in my life suddenly started coming together in a simple, orderly, and joy-filled way.

I came to see that eventually God would give me the understanding I needed. He would answer my questions and bring solutions to the different problems I faced. He would provide *all* the things I needed in life. But God had to remain *first* in my life, regardless of my questions or regardless of whether I understood something or how I felt about it. When I started doing that, all the crazy dots began to connect. Peace and order came to my life. Joy began to fill me, and God became more real, more beautiful, more powerful, and more loving to me than I could ever imagine.

JUST PUT HIM FIRST

This is the God-first life. It's the life God intends you to live. It removes barriers and gives you a simple, sustainable touch point for accessing the freedom and joy that belong to you in Christ. It's far better than just another "app" to marginally improve your life. Beneath the surface are interlocking layers of spiritual depth and supernatural programming that make it revolutionary. But for us, God has made it simple: just put him first.

So, what does this look like, practically? In the single verse of Matthew 6:33, God reveals three key aspects of the new life to which he calls us. Even better, we can look at them as three *promises* if we put him first.

MATTHEW 6:33	PROMISE
"Seek first the kingdom of God."	God promises you a *new family*.
"Seek ... his righteousness."	God promises you a *new life*.
"All these things will be given to you."	God promises you *new freedom*.

The first two—new family and new life—are all about setting the right priorities in our lives and restoring order to the chaos of choices and demands. The third aspect—new freedom—is about experiencing God's blessing.

Let's break this down a bit. First, we enter God's kingdom by coming into his family. This is accomplished through salvation.[14] The way we seek his kingdom is by playing our role in God's family.

Second is God's righteousness, which is his character expressed in his goodness. We enter into God's righteousness by faith in Christ alone, but we seek God's righteousness by ordering our lives according to his patterns so that *our* priorities reflect *his* priorities.

Finally, when we take our place in God's family and order our lives according to his way of doing things, we begin to experience new freedom and breakthroughs in life. We experience a life full of God's favor with all of our needs met because things are in proper order.

You can experience the benefits of a God-first life by seeking his kingdom and his righteousness first. As we close this chapter, I want to drill down on that word, *seeking*. The Greek word Jesus used when he told us to seek God's kingdom and righteousness first is zēteō, which means to search for a final answer to our questions, a final determination. Jesus is saying that we should come to resolution about our life in him, but there's a sense in which we never fully arrive because it's a continual process in going deeper with God.

In the rest of the book, I am going to show you how to do this by inviting you to make some basic, but powerful, decisions. The only question is, *Are you ready?*

ORDER AND BLESSING

Find What It Truly Means
to Put God First

Take delight in the LORD, and he will give you the
desires of your heart.

Psalm 37:4

You know that Johnny Cash song "I've Been Everywhere"?
Sometimes, I feel like that could be my life's anthem. Ever
since my early years in my ministry, I have spent a considerable
amount of time traveling, serving in various mission outreaches,
preaching in various parts of the world, and connecting with
people from all walks of life. No matter where I am or what
group of people I'm talking to, there is one compelling reality
that consistently hits me: We all want the same things.

Whether it's a father wanting a good future for his children,
a young woman looking for a good job, or something much
bigger (like global peace), human beings the world over, of
every race and religion, have similar worries, hopes, dreams,
and desires. We all want a satisfying and productive life. We all
want financial security, meaningful relationships with friends
and family, freedom from worry and fear, and some kind of
legacy to leave behind. Most of all, perhaps, we want love.

Regardless of what we may call it—luck, favor, or fortune—deep down, all of us strive for a life marked by *blessing*. God-first living is the only way to receive the blessing we instinctively seek.

WHAT GETS YOUR BEST?

Most people seem to equate happiness with certain measurable outcomes, using a formula something like this:

$$\text{Right career + plenty of money +}$$
$$\text{right girl/guy + right friends}$$
$$-\text{pain and suffering}$$
$$= \text{happiness}$$

But how often have you seen people who have earnestly followed this formula and yet have continued to struggle to achieve that elusive happiness?

In an interview with *60 Minutes*, New England Patriots star quarterback Tom Brady expressed both surprise and disappointment that his unquestioned fame and success had failed to bring him the satisfaction he craved.

"Why do I have three Super Bowl rings and still think there is something greater out there for me?" Brady wondered aloud to CBS correspondent Steve Kroft. "I mean, maybe a lot of people would say, 'Hey, man, this is what it is.' I've reached my goal, my dream, my life. Me? I think, 'God, it's got to be more than this.'"

Kroft looked him in the eye and asked, "What's the answer?"

"I wish I knew!" responded Brady, shaking his head. "I wish I knew! I love playing football, and I love being the quarterback of this team; but at the same time, I think there are a lot of other parts about me I'm trying to find."[1]

Like Tom Brady, many of us spend most of our time and energy trying to plug the right variables into our "happiness formula" so we can guarantee a good life for ourselves. While I think such an approach has several problems, here's one that does most of the damage: we forget that whatever force has first place in our lives will drive our decisions and shape our futures. No matter how much success, fame, or money we have, if our priorities are out of whack, none of those things will make us happy.

> Whatever force has first place in our lives will drive our decisions and shape our futures.

Whatever has first place in your life directs how you live it. I'm no exception to this rule, and neither are you. So who or what has first place for you? What factor most determines how you choose to live? What causes you to decide where to invest most of your time, money, and energy? How do you select which relationships to nurture and which ones to keep casual? What gets your best?

HAPPINESS IS ABOUT ORDER

I'm going to take a guess about what you're thinking right now. I bet you're waiting for me to drop the happiness-isn't-the-goal-of-life hammer on you, aren't you? Or maybe the God-doesn't-care-about-your-happiness-he-cares-about-your-holiness bomb? Well, sorry to disappoint you. I won't do that, because frankly I don't believe the desire for happiness is a bad thing. Where would we even get the concept of happiness if it didn't come from God?

I'm convinced that in your search for happiness God is not your fiercest opponent, but your greatest ally. But to see things from his perspective, you must master one crucial truth: Happiness isn't about more, better, or greater; it's about order.

Most people think that a great life is all about getting their needs and wants met. They believe that if they can check everything off their "want list," they can settle into a satisfied life. Unfortunately, however, the items on their list never get checked off. In fact, if anything, their list just keeps growing. And if they try to chase down every item on their rapidly expanding list, it ends up consuming them. They wind up trying vainly to figure out why they can't get a handle on it, why they don't ever seem to have "enough," or why what they *do* never seems to satisfy them.

Happiness isn't about more, better, or greater; it's about order.

This is why Jesus told us to seek *first* the kingdom of God and his righteousness. When we do that, "all of these things" will be added to us. He meant that a life of anxiety is never an issue of unmet need but always an issue of disordered priorities. If we get the order right, God promises to meet our needs, with unexpected blessings attached. When we strive to set our *own* priorities, however—when we put God way down the list—we miss out on a life marked by blessing and peace.

"The blessing of the LORD brings wealth, without painful toil for it," says Proverbs.[2] Can you imagine a life without painful toil? The New American Standard translation says that the Lord's blessing makes us rich and he "adds no sorrow to it." How many people do you know who have become rich—but their money has only added to their sorrows? But God wants to bless your life in such a faithful, constant way that whatever "riches" you receive will come to you without added sorrow.

A life of anxiety is never an issue of unmet need but always an issue of disordered priorities ... When order is restored, blessing is released.

When you put God first, you choose a life of proper order that keeps at bay the kind of sorrow, stress, and pain that inundate those who seek riches first. When order is restored, blessing is released. There's nothing wrong with seeking a better financial picture for your family, a better job, and so on, but there is something wrong with seeking these things first. God never asked Tom Brady to stop playing football, any more than he's asking you to stop whatever he's called you to do. He just doesn't want that first in your life. How can God add his blessing to anyone who has chosen to put the things of this life out of their proper order?

One of the great things about the God-first life is that it helps us distinguish between what is truly important and what is merely urgent. A life out of order tends to increase in complexity.

Disorder invites more disorder. The urgent things, those things that demand our immediate attention, typically shout and clamor and scream for first position. But as soon as we take care of them, inevitably another "urgent need" pops up. Ironically, the more we try to get our lives under control through our own efforts, the more we discover that our lives actually control *us*. Meanwhile, the truly important things, the things that will build our lives and restore our souls, go unattended.

But order brings simplicity by showing us what to hold on to and what to release. It brings clarity by bringing our priorities into stronger focus. When we get clear about what's important, we also gain the confidence to tune out whatever competes for our attention, so that we can put our best energy and strength into God and his kingdom *first*.

Putting things into their proper order leads to a balanced, blessed life. And neglecting this order leads to something very, very different.

FORGETTING OUR GREATEST NEED

The summer before my son, Stovie, turned twelve, we went fishing in the Gulf of Mexico with three other guys and their sons. We fished from sunup to sundown and caught our limit every day.

One day we decided to take our boat out a little farther into the gulf so we could fish around the oil rigs. Red snapper love the rigs, and we dads wanted our sons to reel in some of these beauties. So early that morning we set out with all of our gear. We planned to stay out all day, so we went prepared. We packed all kinds of drinks, sandwiches, and snacks, loads of sunscreen, the perfect sunglasses, and all the hats and gear we needed to protect us from the relentless glare of the gulf sun. We also brought every kind of pole and bait we could possibly need. The fish didn't stand a chance! We had everything we needed for a great day of fishing—or so we thought.

We soon caught our limit, and the boys got a chance to haul in some really big fish. After we had fished ourselves to exhaustion, we decided to head back to the camp for dinner. We had just one problem: On our way back, the boat died. As in *chug, chug, chug* . . . nothing.

Out of gas!

Normally we filled the tank with gas before we went out, even if we already had fuel in the tank. But that day, our excitement over having all the right gear, all the right bait, all the right maps and coordinates, the ice, the drinks, the food had made us forget the most important thing—the fuel to make the trip back.

So there we found ourselves, bobbing up and down on the gulf with no other boats in sight, waiting and hoping that someone might sail by and help us get to shore. The whole time I kept thinking, *How in the world did we forget the fuel?* There were so many important things to do to make sure we had a good time on the water, but we forgot the one thing that would make all those other preparations enjoyable and give us peace and security—the fuel. It was the most important thing to remember! It's the one thing we needed most. I can't believe how careless we were!

Eventually another boat did motor by, and its crew offered us some help. We returned to our camp safe and sound. To the kids, it was just another part of the adventure, but all the men knew otherwise. We all recognized the serious danger we had put ourselves in.

When I finally collapsed into bed that night, I had a chance to relive all the events of the day. So many things had competed for our attention as we prepared to visit the rigs. It all got jumbled into a big ball of chaos—trying to get the kids up, fed, dressed, covered in sunscreen, and away from video games. Certainly we had to do all those things, but none of them ranked at the top of our list. None of them deserved the title "most important." Yet in our urgency to get on the boat and push off, we all assumed that someone else had taken care of the fuel. All of us had assumed wrong. Not one of the seasoned fishermen remembered to take onto the boat the one thing most critical to our lives and safety.

In life, as on the gulf, we neglect our greatest need when we forget about order.

A DECISION OF THE WILL

Because our primary focus defines our life, the only way to rightsize our priorities is to change our focus. You and I *must* make a purposeful decision to put God first and then resist the strong urge to put other things in his place—no matter how "important" or even "urgent" they might seem.

While this kind of decision certainly involves our emotions, it is primarily a decision of the *will*. It requires that we say (and mean), "I *will* put God first"—no "maybe" or "possibly" or "if I feel like it" or "if it's easy." And once made, that decision must remain sacred and irrevocable. No going back.

Centuries ago, the apostle Paul made exactly that kind of choice. He made it because he recognized who had called him to make it. He called Christ "the head of the body, the church," and said that Jesus "is the beginning and the firstborn from among the dead, *so that in everything he might have the supremacy*."[3] Paul didn't choose the word "supremacy" as an afterthought. It's a powerful, ultimate kind of word that describes the preeminent authority of God over *all* things.

God must be first. He cannot be second. We yield to a God whose authority brings an empowering blessing, not an oppressive burden. He can satisfy and fulfill us in ways that no person, place, or thing ever will. He created us to find supreme joy only in him, in a profound relationship with the Creator of the universe. He has forever connected our joy and his glory in a bond that no one and nothing can break.

Constant worry, shadowy fear, and a never-ending pursuit of the short-lived pleasures of this life—Jesus has not called you or me to that. Rather, he has called us to live a God-first life, where order is restored so blessing can be released.

"Take delight in the LORD," the Bible counsels, "and he will give you the desires of your heart."[4] If you seek God first in your life—if you will continually reaffirm his supremacy in all you do—he will freely give you all the "things" you could ever truly desire or need.

GOD KNOWS WHAT YOU REALLY NEED

The fifth chapter of Matthew's gospel begins with the Beatitudes, one of the most famous passages in the Bible. It's part of the well-known Sermon on the Mount. In those verses, Jesus addresses our innate desire for happiness, peace, significance, success, identity, comfort, and fulfillment. He doesn't start off by rebuking people for wanting these things. Quite the opposite! Instead, Jesus speaks directly to those desires, challenging us to consider what it takes to have them truly fulfilled.

Jesus does this all through the gospels. He loved to turn the tables and challenge his friends and followers to look at these issues through a different lens, often by giving them an answer that was the *direct opposite* of what they had expected. You want to be great? Make yourself humble.[5] You want to be boss? Learn to be a servant.[6]

Jesus wasn't against happiness—he just redefined how to get it. The things that we fret about having—money, love, material possessions, security, popularity—Jesus says we don't need to strive

> Jesus wasn't against happiness —he just redefined how to get it.

for those things or worry about getting them.[7] In fact, when we strive, we lose. This is the broader context of the God-first life. All the things we worry about getting and losing take a backseat to our pursuit of God. All those things are a by-product of putting God first. Listen to what Jesus says here:

> So do not worry, saying, "What shall we eat?" or "What shall we drink?" or "What shall we wear?" For the pagans run after all these things, and your heavenly Father knows that you need them. But seek first his kingdom and his righteousness, and all these things will be given to you as well.[8]

The things we want and need distract us spiritually with anxiety and worry when we let them take priority in our lives. At some point or another, in some way or another, we all do this. A majority of Americans admit to struggling with anxiety and worry, and there's practically no difference between Christians and non-Christians on this point.[9] *All* of us have these fundamental wants and needs, and all of us are liable to put them first, to worry about them. And the things are not bad in themselves, right? After all, God says he'll give them to us.

In your search for happiness, God is your greatest ally. We were designed to seek an outlet for our gifts and ways to use them to create something of significance. In fact, as we will see shortly, God placed the drive to succeed in the human heart before sin ever entered the world.

Many people read "seek first the kingdom of God" and mistakenly jump to the conclusion that truly seeking God means that material things should no longer matter to us. Jesus did not say that we shouldn't seek those things, but that we shouldn't seek them *first*. There's nothing wrong with money and stuff. The trouble comes when we make acquiring those things our primary goal in life. The primary thing we should wish for, crave, diligently seek is God. And when this proper order is restored, the blessing (the things that will be "given" to us as well) is released into our lives.

WATCH FOR THORNS

I feel blessed that God allows Celebration Church to introduce people to him for the first time every weekend. It keeps me from getting insulated in a church bubble and forgetting what it was like trying to leave my old life behind and build a new life based on completely different values than I used to have. Each Sunday we drop cards on the seats so that people can write down their prayer requests and needs and give thanks for answered prayers. Some of the questions we frequently see remind me of some of the ones I used to ask.

"I was offered a promotion with higher pay, but it means I have to live apart from my family two weeks out of every month. It's hard to turn down in this economy. Should I take it?"

"My boyfriend just asked me to move in with him, and I don't know what to do. Times are tough. It seems like sharing the rent would make things a lot easier. Can you pray for wisdom?"

"My spouse and I fight about money all the time. But she

doesn't know I have a gambling addiction. Should I tell her about running up debt on the secret credit cards I've been hiding? I want to come clean, but I'm afraid it will end our marriage. Can you pray for guidance?"

"I'm seventeen and I'm not married. I just found out I am pregnant. I need to talk to someone, but my parents will be furious when they find out. I have so many regrets now, but I am not sure where to turn. Can you pray for peace?"

"My marriage is so full of pain and brokenness. I am thinking about leaving my husband. Can you pray for me so I can know the right thing to do?"

Each and every one of these situations represents a unique person, known and loved by God. Every person is different, and the details of their stories differ from person to person. But the one thing that I have seen time and again is that when people choose to put God first, it changes the trajectory of their lives in a way that they never thought possible.

That's not to say it's easy. Putting God first doesn't undo bad choices and isn't the path of least resistance. But it's the first and most crucial step toward regaining the peace that has been lost by living in a world where I am at the center of it all.

In the parable of the sower, Jesus describes the fate of the seed that fell among thorns: "Still others, like seed sown among thorns, hear the word; but the worries of this life, the deceitfulness of wealth and the desires for other things come in and choke the word, making it unfruitful."[10] By default, our hearts provide the perfect environmental conditions for thorns to thrive:

cares and anxieties
distractions
pleasures
delusions about wealth
desires for things other than God

This ecosystem of thorn-friendly conditions suffocates the Word, and it becomes fruitless. If you have a lifetime of thorns growing in your soil, sowing one seed will not suddenly cause a harvest of wheat to spring up. Uprooting one thornbush will not dismantle the entire ecosystem. Problems with deeper roots may require more complex solutions. But I can promise you this: unless that first seed is sown and the first thornbush is uprooted, nothing will change.

The way I see it, you are going to spend a lot of energy responding to the problems in your life. Most of that energy will be to no avail because the real issue is not having too many problems but operating from a life that is out of order. We must learn to use energy in a way that will actually bring solutions. Energy invested in a God-first life is not wasted.

FOCUS ON ONE BIG THING

Do you ever watch the nature shows on *Animal Planet* or the *National Geographic Channel*? I do all the time, especially the ones about big cats. It's fascinating to watch lions take on big game like wildebeest, kudu, or water buffalo. Killing these larger animals can be extremely dangerous for the lions. They risk severe injury and even death in their quest for a big meal.

So why not go for smaller, less-threatening prey? There are many options for the lions to choose from. For example, small rodents are abundant in the savannah. Even in lean times, it would be easy for the lions to gorge themselves on small rodents. Why spend so much time, energy, and effort chasing the big game when there are plenty of smaller creatures to go around for the whole pride?

Here's why. The energy that a lion spends chasing a small rodent is greater than the caloric content of that creature. As abundant as the small creatures are, if a lion spent all day chasing them, he could eventually starve himself to death even as he is eating them! To survive, a lion needs to focus on one thing: a *big* meal. If he can just catch the one big thing—the antelope, the wildebeest—the rest of the little things will take care of themselves.

I think the lion is on to something here, and we should pay attention to it. The lion knows what's important, and he stays focused on that one big thing. He's better than scurrying after rodents. And you know what? You're better than that too. You've got a bigger purpose than chasing after all the little things of this life. Unless we focus on the kingdom, we're going to burn ourselves out chasing the little rodents in our lives. The God-first life offers us that focus.

Is the trajectory of your life the one you hoped for? Is it a path you want to continue along, or do you wish you had the power to stop it and redirect it? Regardless of your past mistakes and poor choices, you can decide how you respond from this point on. The choice is yours—no one else's—and it all comes down to the simple, sustainable principle of order.

Once you've decided to make God a priority in your life, the next decision is to make his family a priority.

PART 2

NEW FAMILY

Seek first *his kingdom* and his righteousness, and all these things will be given to you as well.

Matthew 6:33

ADOPTED INTO GOD'S FAMILY

Understand Your Position as a Member of God's Family

> You are no longer strangers and outsiders ... You are members of God's family.
>
> *Ephesians 2:19, NIrV*

I have friends who adopted a boy from Africa. (To respect the family's privacy, let's call him Nathan.) When Nathan's new parents came to the orphanage, he was excited.

Can you imagine? A three-year-old little boy who had never had a family before—never had a mom or a dad, never had brothers or sisters. Nathan was thrilled to be part of a family. After the adoption was finalized, there were legal documents that said exactly who Nathan was and who his new family was. His place in his new family was secure. But I'd be lying if I said there wasn't a challenging period of adjustment when they got home. That's because there's a big difference between *position* and *function*.

It took a long time for Nathan to know how to fit in. All the little roles and rules that kids naturally pick up over the years were hard for him to adapt to. It took him time to get used to being

35

part of a family, to know how it works and how he was expected to behave. Although Nathan's position in his new family was secure, he struggled with function. But the loving work of his adoptive parents and siblings helped bring up this child in his new family, and eventually he began taking on the characteristics of his new family.

It's the same with us. If you're a Christian, you are adopted into God's family. And it's the loving work of the family—the church—to help us grow and take on the characteristics of our new family. Just as Nathan was created to live in the context of a loving family, so we are created for fellowship with God and with one another in the church, in the family of God. But also like Nathan, sometimes that adjustment is challenging. We have our position in the family, but we also have a function, a role to play, and we are never truly settled and satisfied in the family until we start to live out the role God has for us.

Knowing you have a function is different from being willing and able to perform it. In the orphanage Nathan developed all sorts of behaviors and coping strategies that helped him survive in his environment. But when that environment changed, those behaviors and strategies became counterproductive.

Same thing with the church. The life and habits I learned before coming to Christ didn't always serve me well when I carried them over into my new family. We sometimes have competing family values at play—an old nature and a new nature, as the apostle Paul talked about in Romans 6 and 7. But when we decide to join God's family, we're deciding to let go of our old patterns and instead to adopt God's way of doing things.

The God-first life is not meant to be lived out on your own. In fact, it really can't be done. We're meant to live with God and enjoy our blessed position in his family.

When we come into God's family through Jesus, the church becomes our primary family. Don't get me wrong. Your biological family is still your primary *earthly* family. In fact, when you understand your place in God's family, it will help you love, lead, and be a greater blessing to your earthly family. Loving our spouses, caring for our kids, being good sons and daughters—all of this comes as a by-product of making God's family your primary family. Joy is one of the great blessings in being part of God's family, and you can bring that joy to your earthly family.

> The God-first life is not meant to be lived out on your own. In fact, it really can't be done.

Now, I know you may have issues with church, and they may be well founded. We've all had our disappointments over legalism, hypocrisy, or even worse problems in churches we have known. But what I'm asking is that you set all that aside for the moment and consider the church in light of what God intended it to be. Even with its imperfections, the body of Christ is the context we need if we are going to successfully learn to put God first in our lives and experience the benefits that come from it.

YOUR POSITION IS SECURE

Before we get into these new patterns, I think it's important to stress something. To fully experience the God-first life, you absolutely must come to understand God's unmistakable love for you and complete acceptance of you. The moment you place your faith in Christ, you are born into his family and secure a permanent position in it. You cannot go far in your life of faith until you come to understand and embrace this amazing reality. Your position in God's family is secure.

A few years ago, I had the opportunity to bring Kerri and the kids along with me for a ministry trip in Europe. I was excited when our schedule opened up enough to visit Wemyss Castle in Fife, Scotland. For several decades now, my aunt and grandparents have been researching our family ancestry, and it surprised them to find that the Wemyss (pronounced *Weems*) family belongs to one of the oldest in Scotland, the McDuff clan. Throughout the centuries, the Wemyss family established several villages surrounding its castle and amassed impressive holdings of land and resources. I just had to drop in. *Who knows?* I thought. *Maybe my long-lost relatives have some unclaimed inheritance waiting for me!*

When we finally arrived at the estate after an hour's drive from St. Andrews, we felt a little disappointed to find that we could not go inside. Unlike most historical castles in Scotland, Wemyss Castle has residents—the Wemyss family, in fact. This castle serves as their private home. And, as the groundskeeper politely informed us, "the public" cannot traipse through. I tried to explain to him that we were not "the public," since we were family, but he was unimpressed. He kindly redirected us to the Wemyss Castle Gardens and explained the history of the site.

As the groundskeeper guided us through the gardens, I noticed that he referred to the current owners as "Mr." and "Mrs.," not "Lord" and "Lady," as he did when referring to their ancestors. So I asked if Scotland still had earls and dukes.

"Of course we do!" he said. "But Mr. and Mrs. Wemyss may no longer be called by their titles."

It turns out that a conflict had once erupted over the throne of Scotland, and the Wemyss family chose the losing side. After the fight was over, the king restored the family lands, but not the titles. As a perpetual reminder of their shameful rebellion against the crown, the Wemyss family and all their descendants lost the right to be called by their former noble rank. Removing their titles meant their transgression would follow them forever. I'm so thankful that Jesus came to do just the *opposite*. When we come into God's family through Christ, our transgressions are removed forever. We are justified. It is *just* as though we have never sinned. All of our past, present, and future sins are totally forgiven forever. Your position in God's family is secure.

Let me ask you a question: How secure could *you* feel in a family if you knew you did not have a permanent position there but that you could be stripped of your identity at any moment? One of the key things to understand about your relationship with God is that your position in his family is secure. But maybe like my friend's boy Nathan, you need to be reminded often that you belong.

PERMANENT MEMBERS

Over many years, I have spoken with countless believers who struggle in nearly every aspect of living out their faith because they fail to get this crucial truth. They think there is an agenda with God or a catch to his love. They never learned that when they became members of God's family, they became *permanent* members. Thus they carry around shame and guilt like an ever-present reminder of past failures and poor choices. They believe that God accepts them when they do well and rejects them when they do poorly. Every time they sin, they imagine that God despises them, rejects them, and has taken away their position within his family.

Because these misled men and women try to base their relationship with God on their own performance, they remain caught in a deeply discouraging cycle:

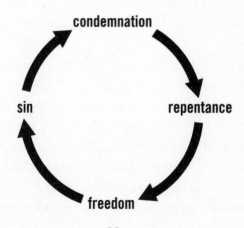

39

This cycle repeats, and they lose any momentum they might once have gained on their trajectory of spiritual growth. As a result, their relationship with God plunges into fear, guilt, shame, and timidity. Yes, by God's grace they still experience moments of freedom and power, but these moments get overwhelmed by many (and frequently longer) periods of spiritual dryness and apathy.

Listen, this is not anywhere *close* to the abundant life Jesus intends for us to have! Get this image instead:

> Blessed is the man one trusts in the LORD,
>   whose confidence is in him.
> They will be like a tree planted by the water
>   that sends out its roots by the stream.
> It does not fear when heat comes;
>   its leaves are always green.
> It has no worries in a year of drought
>   and never fails to bear fruit.[1]

That's a picture of the God-first life. The tree (that's us) is firmly planted by the water's edge. Imagine the shoreline as the church, and the stream as the refreshing current of the Holy Spirit. When that's your life, the troubles of life can come and problems in your own heart can come, but you'll never fail to be fruitful because the church supports you and the Spirit refreshes you.

Let me tell you: That's your life — or it can be. But a lot of us don't feel like that firmly planted tree. We feel like tumbleweed, dry and blowing around in the winds of life. It doesn't have to be that way. How do I know? Let me explain by changing the image we are working with.

God loves unconditionally, regardless of our performance. Why? Because he relates to us through the finished work of Jesus Christ on the cross. The letter to the Hebrews beautifully describes the work of Christ that secures forever our place in God's family:

> When this priest [Christ] had offered *for all time one sacrifice* for sins, he sat down at the right hand of God, and since that time he waits for his enemies to be made his footstool. For by *one sacrifice* he has *made perfect forever* those who are *being made holy*.[2]

Let that truth sink in! Jesus offered *one* sacrifice, *one* time. One sacrifice for *all* sins, plural—your sin, my sin, your family's sins, your children's, your grandchildren's, all the future sins that will ever be committed. The cross paid for every one of them! The finished work of the cross has created a safe place, a *permanent family home*, for all who believe.

A VALUABLE FUNCTION

As a part of God's team and a member of his family, your permanent *position* comes with an important *function*. It's one thing to become a member of a championship-caliber team; it's quite another to actually suit up and play. Without eagerly engaging with your new function in God's kingdom, you cannot fully experience the blessings wrapped up in a God-first life.

When my son, Stovie, was about five years old, he played on a junior soccer team. It was his first team sport, and I was pumped to watch him play his first game. We dressed him in all his gear: the jersey, the shin guards, the cleats, a mouth guard, and the long socks. He had everything he needed. We took tons of pictures of him, packed an ice chest so we could make it a family day at the field, and headed out to watch the game.

Not that there was much game happening. When five-year-olds play soccer, not a lot of actual soccer gets played. Instead, you see a lot of sitting on the field, running in the wrong direction, carrying the ball, colliding into other kids, crying, talking to friends, and all that.

But what happens if a guy like Jack McBean of the Los Angeles Galaxy were to do the same thing? Not cute or funny at all. Imagine if McBean showed up, but instead of playing, he sat down in midgame to pick at some grass on the field or refused to play until he felt happy with the color of his cleats. That wouldn't be cute—it would be crazy! We expect grownups to act like grownups. For kids, just making the team earns them a trophy. But on professional teams, making the team means you have a function that you must fulfill.

Being part of God's family involves both place and function. God gives us a position in his family so that we can have a role in it. We gain our place in God's kingdom family by faith in Christ, but we seek his kingdom first by fulfilling our function in his family. Many believers disconnect at exactly this point—and that disconnection explains why they don't fully experience the blessing of God. They don't understand that while position gets them on the team, function gets them in the game. Belonging comes first, but now it's time to play ball.

Maybe another analogy will help. In my family I have two positions: *husband* and *father*. These words identify not only my place in my family but also my functions. My marriage certificate and kids' birth certificates prove my position. But that doesn't mean a whole lot if I don't also fulfill the functions of the husband and father in my family.

Imagine if, on the day Kerri and I got married, I had said "I do" and then walked back down the aisle, got into my truck, and drove off saying, "Okay, well, we're married now, so I guess I'll check back in on Christmas, Easter, and maybe on Mother's Day if my mom forces me to come. If I start feeling guilty, or if I don't have anything better to do, I will stop by. See ya later!"

Any woman in her right mind would stop such a marriage before it even got started. The marriage license and the wedding vows secure my place as a husband. And that position gives me access to the benefits of being married to Kerri—the marriage bed, the love and support of a faithful wife, the best braised short ribs on the planet—but it doesn't fulfill my commitment to her. My commitment to Kerri is not expressed in my position as her husband but in my function as her husband.

> Think of it like this: Position gives us access, but function gives us impact.

Position and function are intertwined. We cannot function without position, but our position must carry over into function. Since Jesus is our Savior, Lord, and King, our primary family is in his kingdom. And Jesus the King calls on us to fulfill our proper roles in his kingdom family. Both function and position are critical for experiencing the God-first life. Think of it like this: Position gives us access, but function gives us impact. Who doesn't want a life of impact? Jack McBean has a jersey and a place on the field, but he's got to play his position if he wants to score.

GENUINE TRANSFORMATION

The weather in Jacksonville is wonderful, and I'm out and about a lot. It seems like every time when I'm at the beach or drop by my favorite Starbucks, I run into people from our church. I always find it interesting to hear their stories of how they found our church, how it has impacted them, and what God has done in their lives. I hear those stories a lot, and I love hearing them.

But I also often get a different kind of story, one I *don't* enjoy hearing. Almost always it goes something like this:

"Hi, Pastor Stovall! I've been wanting to meet you. I go to your church, or I did (*insert embarrassed blush here*). Well, I mean, I haven't been going as much as I should be. See, I got this job, and I have to work Sundays. And I recently started dating this guy, and he doesn't feel like going to church at night. So anyway (*cue tears*), long story short, a lot of bad things have been going on and (*more tears*) my life is kind of a mess right now, and (*full blown sob*) can you pray for me?"

We usually end up praying, right then and there. I always give the same advice: "God loves you and wants to help you, but you need to truly put him first. Stop trying to just 'add' God to your life. Our lives become a mess when they are out of order. Make God your first priority. I'll see you back in church on Sunday."

Sooner or later, that person usually walks up to me after some Sunday service and tells me how that day became a key turning point. The breakthrough didn't come after hours of counseling or through reading a stack of books I'd recommended. The turning point came simply when the person decided to make God his or her first priority, a decision that initiated transformation in the person's life, relationships, and circumstances.

PLANTED IN GOOD SOIL

Throughout the Bible, the church is described in three main ways: a family, a house, and a body. Each of these images emphasizes different aspects of what it means to be part of the fellowship of believers. Family speaks to community and belonging. Body speaks to health and function. House speaks to design, pattern, and purpose. But one thing that all of these images have in common is that they refer to many working as one.

Another image the Bible uses is that of a garden. There is perhaps no better picture of the benefits of being planted in the local church than Psalm 92:

> The righteous will flourish like a palm tree,
>   they will grow like a cedar of Lebanon;

planted in the house of the LORD,
they will flourish in the courts of our God.
They will still bear fruit in old age,
they will stay fresh and green,
proclaiming, "The LORD is upright;
he is my Rock, and there is no wickedness in him."[3]

Notice that the righteous are compared to palm trees and cedars of Lebanon. When we read the names of those trees, we might not think much of them. But to the ancient Palestinians, these trees communicated specific imagery. These particular plants were chosen to describe the righteous person because of the unique characteristics they possess. Both types of trees were beautiful, desirable, and highly prized for their contribution to that ancient culture.

Palm trees were the most common trees in ancient Palestine. Not only were they beautiful and stately, but the various parts of the palm tree were used in nearly every aspect of daily life. The fruit of the palm tree was a staple of the Palestinian diet. Its leaves were made into everything from baskets to fences. The juice of the fruit made arrack, a common drink, and the fibers that held the palm fronds together were separated and woven into ropes. Palm trees speak of usefulness and fruitfulness.

The cedars of Lebanon trees grow among the snow, near the highest parts of Lebanon. Because they are resistant to disease and decay, they are durable, long-lived, and enormous in size. These cedars are evergreen trees that give off a fresh aroma. The cedar speaks of majesty, stability, durability, and incorruptibility.

Useful, *fruitful*, *stable*, *durable*, and *incorruptible*. That is what it means to flourish in the context of this passage. Who wouldn't want those words to describe their life?

Everyone wants to flourish in life—flourishing families, careers, finances, and health. There is absolutely nothing wrong with that. I believe God wants those things for us too. But we must understand that before we can flourish, we have to be planted. *"Planted* in the house of the LORD, *they will flourish* in the courts of our God." Not many people want to "plant." That's not to say we don't want to be "used." Everybody wants God to use them to change the world. So what do we do to change the world? We take "gifts" tests, we seek our purpose, and we look for ways to use our gifts and talents. We start blogs, nonprofits, new ministries, new careers, new relationships, and churches. We will do almost anything to be used by God—except stay planted.

The local church is the soil necessary for your life to flourish. It is the foundation of a growing, vibrant, healthy spiritual life. People are like acorns. Unless they get into the soil, their hard outer shell remains tough and there's no life there. But get them into the soil, and that shell softens. New life sprouts and grows.

God has a purpose and plan for each individual person whom he calls into his family. This is what we call God's personal will for your life. When we join with the local church, we are stepping into the design and pattern best structured to impact our local communities. It is in the context of the local church that you experience the God-first life!

I notice that young believers in particular spend loads of energy worrying about their purpose and God's personal will for their lives. What most people overlook—and not just young people—is that God has a revealed will for your life as well as a personal will for it. God's revealed will is written for us in his Word. We don't have to pray to understand that part of God's will, and we don't have to spend energy trying to discover it— it's already there. All we have to do is obey it! We will not have clarity and confidence in living out God's personal will until we are in obedience to his revealed will in his Word. Being planted in God's house is part of his revealed will.

There are several commands in the New Testament that we are incapable of obeying until we are planted in a local church. And don't forget that these commands are also blessings. If we follow the apostle Paul's direction to "carry each other's burdens,"[4] sometimes we'll be giving and other times we'll be receiving the benefit. Either way, we cannot experience the God-first life without being planted in a local church.

STAYING PLANTED

When I first moved to Florida, I was preoccupied with palm trees. One of the first things I did when we bought our first home in Jacksonville was buy a highly sensitive type of palm tree called a Robellini palm. It's really better suited for the warmer climates of south Florida. I just wanted to go as tropical as I could get, and the Robellini seemed like the perfect palm tree to get me there.

The Robellini started its brief and tragic life in the back corner of the yard near a water feature we had installed. It looked healthy and tropical the whole summer and fall. But once the first hard freeze came, it turned brown overnight. Determined to give the tree its best chance for survival, I tried moving it to different places throughout the yard. First, I moved it to the other corner amid the elm trees. When that didn't work, I moved it to the edge of the patio. When that move proved futile, I moved it to the bed that ran along the back of the house, hoping that the heat from the house would give it a little extra insulation from the cold.

In spite of my determined efforts, I could see that the Robellini was not likely to make it through the winter. In a last rally to save it, I called a botanist friend of mine over to take a look at the plant. "What can I do to save this tree?" I asked him. "Can I add something to the soil? Can I put heat lamps on it?"

My friend explained to me that the soil was not the problem. The soil was fine. And even though the cold may have caused a problem at one time, I had a different issue on my hands now. In trying to find the perfect environment for the Robellini to flourish, I had uprooted and replanted it so many times that it had missed its growing season and failed to thrive. The growing season had passed and the tree would not be able to put down roots strong enough to sustain it through the winter.

The same thing happens with church. Many people never flourish and experience fulfillment of their potential for kingdom purposes because they see "planting" as optional. In some cases they may even see planting themselves in the house of God as something that will hold them back from reaching their potential. That's like saying the root systems of an oak tree are holding it back from reaching its potential. The opposite is actually true—the roots are the reason the oak tree lives up to its potential!

In the life of every plant there are seasons for dormancy, seasons for growth, and seasons for harvest. All of them have a crucial role to play in the plant's fruitfulness. Even when there is no visible fruit on the branches of the tree, everything in the tree is gearing up for that one moment when the fruit is perfectly ripe and ready to be harvested. It's the nature of the tree to multiply itself in harvest. So in the dormant seasons, the tree is resting and storing up energy for the harvest. During the growing season, when the leaves are green but no fruit has started growing, the tree is taking in sunlight and water to create food and nutrients for the harvest. Then finally, the moment that the tree was made for happens. The fruit is borne, and it ripens to perfection.

Somehow I think we have come to expect every season to be one of harvest. Of course we know that's not realistic, but when we can't see visible progress, we start getting restless. We think something must be wrong with the soil, so we uproot to find the perfect environment for our potential to flourish. But every time we uproot and replant, we interrupt part of our life cycle in the house of God. By the time we reacclimate ourselves to our new environment, we have missed the growth season, and yet we wonder why we never see our gifts used to their fullest capacity.

Kerri and I recently moved the family into a new home, one that features a Robellini palm that—unlike my last plant—has stayed put since it was originally planted. It's massive. What stays put has the chance to grow. Uprooting is the enemy of fruitfulness. If we want to be palms and cedars—useful, fruitful, stable, durable, and incorruptible—we have to stay planted.

BUILDING GOD'S CHURCH

It's common to hear people talk about loving God but not liking church. I understand how people can feel that way. I have had negative experiences in church too—and some of them have been at the church I pastor! But we shouldn't let that keep us from becoming a functional member of God's family.

I have had terrible experiences at all kinds of places—restaurants, movie theaters, clothing stores, and airports (*oh, the negative experiences I have had in airports!*). But never once have I walked out of an airport and said, "That's it! I am never flying again. I will never again darken the doors of another airplane." But we do that with church, don't we?

The thing is, God and the church are a package deal. The church is the family of God, and local churches make up the clans or tribes of that family. Just like our natural families, churches fall somewhere on a sliding scale between healthy and dysfunctional. When churches are healthy, they are powerful forces for good in our lives. They help us mature in the context of community; they help us release our potential; and they are a place where truth and love meet to create a safe place for change.

The church was God's idea, not humanity's idea. It has taken on various forms and expressions throughout the ages. Like any institution made up of imperfect people, it is susceptible to corruption. But the church still remains God's plan A for getting the message of the gospel out to the world and even making it come alive daily in our hearts. There's no plan B. We're all God's got, and that includes the broken, dysfunctional ones too. But that's all of us, right? Any church we join is going to be imperfect because it's full of people like us.

Jesus is building his church. It's the only thing he ever said he was going to build: "On this rock I will build my church, and the gates of Hades will not overcome it."[5]

"My church" is possessive language. Not just any church, a church, or some church, but "my church." The church is the bride of Christ and God's chosen vehicle for displaying his glory and carrying his message. The church is why Christ died and rose again. As Paul says, "Christ loved the church and gave himself up for her."[6]

When we become believers in Christ, we are adopted into God's family positionally, and nothing can ever change that. Through salvation you have access to the grace of God, and you will spend eternity with him. Church membership has no impact on that aspect of your faith. But you cannot be a fully functioning member of his family without being planted in the local church.

DOING LIFE TOGETHER

Be Transformed through Community

> Every day they continued to meet together ... They broke bread in their homes and ate together with glad and sincere hearts.
>
> *Acts 2:46*

When I made the decision to put God first in my life, it was like stepping through a doorway into an unfamiliar room. As the door to my old life closed behind me, I eagerly sought to familiarize myself with this new room and its configuration — to learn how to navigate the floor plan of my new life. I embraced all the recommendations of my Christian friends. I got planted in a local church, gave my heart over to worship and instruction, and committed myself to the study of God's Word with great eagerness to see the move of God in my life.

But not long into my new God-first life, I realized that something integral to my growth was missing. Don't get me wrong. I was going to church, and I had lots of good friends and influences in my life. But I didn't have a place where I could really talk about personal things I was struggling with or the deeper questions I had about God. These questions and struggles I was trying to figure out on my own, and I had no deep connections with other believers with whom I could discuss these issues or seek answers to my questions.

Then one day someone asked me to join a men's group. There was a guy who was a leader in the church and had a small group of guys over to his house once a week for several months. He would always have something to share, and we were free to ask any questions. And there were a lot of tough questions. We had guys there from broken homes. We had stuff in our pasts that we needed to sort out. In addition, there were hard theological questions.

I saw it as an opportunity to connect and grow, and I was right. Just a couple of weeks into my participation in the group, I began to see pieces of the puzzle of faith fall into place. I grew in my knowledge and understanding of the grace of God. Dots were connected. Questions were answered. Strong relationships and friendships were formed. I grew by leaps and bounds as a young man of God.

Do you know that even now, twenty years later, I still have a relationship with most of these men? So powerful was their impact on my early walk of faith that they are now permanently stitched into the fabric of my life. Relationships in the body of Christ are *that* important, and they can only be created and sustained through purposeful connection.

The journey of life was never intended for us to walk alone. We must stop trying to do it all by ourselves. Isolation only brings pain, hurt, and decay. Doing the journey by yourself is not God's best for you. That's not a part of putting God first. He has something better in mind for us by way of fellowship, community, and connection. As we do life together with others who love Jesus, it helps us put the priorities in our lives in the right order and open us to the blessings God desires to give.

WHAT A FLOURISHING COMMUNITY LOOKS LIKE

If you want to see what a flourishing church looks like, turn to the book of Acts. They flourished because they understood the keys to true community and did things the way God intended. There was order, and therefore God released the blessing, so much so that we still view them as a model today.

> Those who accepted his message were baptized, and about three thousand were added to their number that day.
>
> They devoted themselves to the apostles' teaching and to fellowship, to the breaking of bread and to prayer. Everyone was filled with awe at the many wonders and signs performed by the apostles. All the believers were together and had everything in common. They sold property and possessions to give to anyone who had need. Every day they continued to meet together in the temple courts. They broke bread in their homes and ate together with glad and sincere hearts, praising God and enjoying the favor of all the people. And the Lord added to their number daily those who were being saved.[1]

The church of Acts was a true community, and there are four main characteristics that made it that way.

1. *They were committed to putting God first.* The church of Acts was first and foremost devoted to their relationship with God and the cause of Christ. From this devotion flowed their loyalty to each other as they did life together. Clearly there were moments of difficulty, sacrifice, and pain as they took part in spreading the gospel (witness the persecution of Acts 8), but they had each other to share the weight of that. Any time you are doing life together with other people, there are bound to be conflicts and challenges. We're talking about people, remember? But they stayed faithful to God first. This is the best and only trustworthy foundation for true community.

2. *They were filled with the Spirit.* Something powerful takes place when believers gather together. Jesus says, "Where two or three gather in my name, there am I with them."[2] God reveals

more of who he is and what he has planned for us through fellowship with other believers. Until you have a moment with Jesus in the midst of true fellowship, there will be parts of your life and purpose that will remain hidden from you. There are certain things that God has ordained to release and reveal to you in the context of relationship. It could be during a conversation with a friend or during group prayer. During these times, God fills us with his hope, strength, and joy and draws us together with one another for purpose.

3. *They did life together.* Every family has good times and bad times. But the strongest of families stick together through it all. What I've noticed among believers in the church is that most of us don't mind spending a "convenient" amount of time with each other. It could be a brief conversation or a one-time gathering. We might offer some quick counsel or advice and finish with "See ya later!" But real community and life change happen when you go the distance, when you're in it for the long haul. This is where the relationships go from hovering on the surface to gaining real depth. Those are the relationships that will make a real difference in our lives. When you make the decision to be truly devoted to the relationships God has placed in your life, you will start to see a huge difference and you won't want to live life doing things on your own anymore. You'll get to the point where you actually want to do life together with others. This is the way God intended it to be.

> In the God-first life, *when order is restored, blessing is released.*

4. *They were added to.* When God looks down from heaven and sees a healthy church, he blesses it. He sends more people, to be discipled and taught, adding to the strength of the relationships already there. Remember, in the God-first life, *when order is restored, blessing is released.* God wants to see unity in us first before he adds to us. God wants to see fellowship and

community—first—and then he adds to us. Healthy, living things grow and multiply, and God's family is no different. In fact, in a world where authentic community is so scarce, it is one of the things that makes us naturally attractive to the hurting, lonely people who need help with their mess (even if they don't know it).

The church of Acts shows us the way to true community. They were the body of Christ, and so can we be.

LIFE IN THE BODY

In the previous chapter we compared the church to a garden. I mentioned that there are other pictures the Bible uses to explain the church, including the body.[3] I've always liked this image because its meaning is so obvious. The ear can't taste, the fingers can't see, and the nose can't hear. Each part of the human body has a purpose and serves to help other parts function. How can the feet function without the legs and knees operating properly to enable movement? Each part is critical and brings strength to the others.

The body of Christ is no different. We need each other. Each of us has a unique purpose and function in the family of God. We can accomplish this only by connecting with other believers.

The relationships we can have in and with the body of Christ form a community that we need to invest in beyond Sunday morning services. Like being filled with the Spirit, or worshiping, or taking time for devotion, it's continual in the God-first life. If your interaction with the body that you are a part of is limited to Sunday morning services, you are missing out on an entire range of experiences that God designed to enrich and strengthen your life in him. Even when you are faithful to weekend services, you will find there are some things that are critical in your relationship with God that cannot be accomplished or cleaned up in weekend services. There are some things we can only clean up by getting in the trenches with each other and doing life together day by day.

1. *Community helps you grow.* There are many different ways that community can help you grow, but it can be summed up by Solomon in Proverbs, "As iron sharpens iron, so a friend sharpens a friend."[4] When we are engaged in community from the body of Christ, a natural by-product is that we sharpen each other to be more effective for the kingdom and more like Jesus. The more people you surround yourself with, the "sharper" you get, helping each other move forward in life and advancing in every area. Isn't the goal of discipleship to become more like Jesus Christ and more effective for the kingdom of God?

2. *Community helps you through hard times.* We will all face hard times. It's not a matter of *whether* hard times will come; it's a matter of *when* they will come. Life has a way of stacking on the pain, and sometimes it can just seem relentless! What I've learned is that in some of the most difficult times, our enemy will try harder than ever to isolate us. But thankfully God has given us each other as the body of Christ and a community of believers to help each other through those times. "Be happy with those who are happy, and weep with those who weep."[5] A community brings the strength and love of several, all stepping in to help when needed.

When times are bad, we need friends who will be there for us and help us keep a God-first perspective. And when times are great, we need friends to celebrate with and praise God with for all he's done. Friends like that can be found only in the body of Christ. Whether in seasons of good or bad, we are intended to share life with others. The love and strength of community adds to our lives something that is unmatched.

3. *Community helps you heal.* James says, "Confess your sins to each other and pray for each other so that you may be healed."[6]

Notice that this Scripture says confessing our sins one to another brings *healing,* not *salvation.* Salvation comes only through faith in Jesus Christ. But we should not forget or underestimate the healing power of confession.

Confession to God brings forgiveness, but confession to a trusted friend can also bring healing. Confession is for our healing and protection. It gets things out into the light, for one. It's only natural to try to hide things that we are ashamed of. But what most people don't realize is that we actually give more power to sin if we keep it secret. Secrecy produces shame, and shame is like adding gas to the power of sin in our lives. The only antidote to the power of secrecy, shame, and sin is confession.

When you confess to someone a weight you have been carrying, it's like a thousand pounds are lifted off your shoulders. The enemy's lies and condemnation are no longer effective. You will discover that we all have the same struggles, just in different forms, and that confession is medicine to our soul. It is so liberating. I have trusted friends in my life whom I talk to weekly, where I can get out on the table anything that I might be struggling with or feeling guilty about. I have learned that when I'm alone, I lose; when I'm together with others, I win.

This brings us to another way confession brings healing, namely, by placing us in a context of relational accountability to others. Truth sets us free but patient endurance matures us

> People don't *fall* into community; they pursue it.

and helps us to walk out the freedom we have experienced. So many of us continually struggle with sin and the pain and regret that comes with it because we keep going around the same mountain over and over. Most of the time we could hold on to freedom if we would just go to a good friend and ask him or her to hold us accountable in our struggles. In the context of accountability, you have someone praying for you, and James adds, "The prayer of a righteous person is powerful and effective."[7] We all need people praying for us in areas of weakness in our lives.

We all need to be in community with each other, whether it is for growth, healing, or helping each other through hard times. None of us can finish strong without it. A God-first circle of friends and fellow believers will help you press through, so decide to make it a part of your life. People don't *fall* into community; they pursue it.

How? One practical way is through small groups within your church.

WORKING FROM COMMON INTERESTS

Most churches create environments where community can take place outside of their weekend services. This is usually accomplished through small groups. At Celebration Church, we like to call them "connect groups." Whatever your local church calls them, groups like this are designed to help you build relationships with others while growing spiritually and getting the help or healing you need. This is a great starting point for getting connected into the community of your local church.

Groups can follow many different formats, but considering the diverse interests we have, it's best to try focusing on the ones we share in common. We've learned that there are generally five areas that can naturally draw people together, and churches or individual Christians can build groups around any of these: faith, family, finance, freedom, and fitness.

Some will find a prayer group or Bible study super helpful in growing their *faith* and coming together. As you learn alongside other believers, community and relationship are a natural by-product. People who learn together naturally grow closer together.

Others are facing the pressing needs of raising a *family* and all the challenges that life's different stages bring. Learning how to navigate those changes according to biblical principles can save us a lot of time, pain, and energy. Finding or starting a group with this focus can bring people together and create the kind of community for mutual support and encouragement.

Whether it's individually or within a family, *finances* can be one of the greatest areas of stress in our lives. Of all the divorces that take place, a majority are due to financial issues. It doesn't have to be this way. The Bible has a lot to say about stewarding our finances, and groups or a class dedicated to teaching and counseling through these principles will go a long way to helping a church flourish.

Just as we talked earlier about relearning patterns and breaking old habits, small groups with a focus on *freedom* can help you overcome certain patterns and behaviors that are keeping you from moving forward in your walk with God. If you're struggling to overcome something, look for a group that will lead you down the path of healing and health in that area. As you learn to apply the truths of the freedom you have in Christ, you will experience the transformation only he can bring.

Finally, part of doing life together is having fun together! At Celebration Church, we've seen that our *fitness* groups have actually been a great way of reaching out to others. Some of the people in our church started coming to Celebration as a result of what they saw take place in our athletic groups. When they saw believers in action, having fun together while focusing on their faith, it opened the door to a new level of community. These groups also include exercise and dance classes. Each group included a spiritual devotion component as well.

However your church does it, the point is to get connected. You can't do the Christian life alone. "Christianity is essentially a social religion," John Wesley once preached. "To turn it into a solitary religion, is indeed to destroy it."[8]

'S HOLDING YOU BACK?

d that many who understand the value that the Christian community brings still don't make an effort to connect. Why? If you've been reluctant to share your life with other believers, consider whether one of these reasons might be your problem.

For starters, we're busy. I've said it; you've said it: *I just don't have time for any extra commitments. I have enough going on in my life.* But listen: deep community will not happen if we value busyness over relationships. Meaningful relationships and friendships are what makes life rich. If we want to experience the benefits of community, we have to invest in the communities we belong to. It's a two-way street. I find that people can get so disappointed because the church was not "there for them" in their moment of crisis. But if we are not investing in others within the community, we won't be in a position to reap the benefits of the community in our time of need.

Here's a difficult one: laziness. *I just don't have the energy to connect with others,* some think. *I already have friends through social media—why do I need more?* We live in a technological age where we can "connect" with many people and acquire many "friends" through social media. Yet this creates a great deal of loneliness. That's because Facebook friends and Twitter followers, whom you can communicate with so easily at the tap of your fingertips, don't give you true community, real connection. True community occurs face to face. It takes intentional time and effort. To walk in deep relationships with other men and women will require energy, but the rewards you reap will be well worth the effort.

Unrealistic expectations are also a problem. *I tried a small group, but I didn't feel like anybody cared about me. Nobody talked to me. I didn't find my best friend in the first week. It's just not for me.* Er, wrong. Why don't you try this: give and sow whatever it is that you want and desire.

If you want a lot of encouragement, sow a lot of encouragement.

If you want to have a great friend in your life, sow being a great friend to someone else.

If you want someone to listen to what's going on in your world right now, sow by listening to somebody else.

If you want trustworthy friends who won't gossip behind your back, sow by being a trustworthy friend.

It's actually all in the giving of what you want.

The reason connection and fellowship with other believers are so important is because our growth and healing are on the line. Community is where God shapes us into the image of Christ. But it will take effort and commitment. Everybody wants the benefits of community, but few people experience it, because so many get stopped by one of the hurdles named above (or perhaps others). True community is valuable because it comes at a price. It doesn't happen overnight or by accident. True community must be pursued, fought for, and prioritized. To experience it in its fullest and richest form means that we will have to surrender our rights and sacrifice for it sometimes.

Living in true community takes time. There is no way around it. It requires longevity and endurance over time, one step at a time. It's not a race you can run in a few seconds, or even a marathon you can run in a few hours. It will take years of doing life together to build the spiritual relationships you want to have. That's God's way of building his church and forming Christ in us.

If depth, joy, beauty, fullness, healing, and knowledge of Christ are all at stake, then community is worth the time and effort given to find those things. You will need this community for the new life ahead of you.

PART 3

NEW LIFE

Seek first his kingdom and *his righteousness*, and all these things will be given to you as well.

Matthew 6:33

DON'T HIDE YOUR TREASURE

Be Filled by the Holy Spirit to Live God's Way

Therefore, if anyone is in Christ, the new creation
has come: The old has gone, the new is here!
2 Corinthians 5:17

George Owen Walton was born on May 15, 1907, in Rocky
Mount, Virginia. As an estate appraiser, he had first dibs on rare
coins, guns, jewelry, stamps, and books, and he built up quite a
collection. When Walton had an opportunity to purchase one
of only five 1913 Liberty Head nickels ever minted, he jumped
at the chance. He paid $3,750 for the treasure in 1945 and told
his family that it was worth a fortune. But after Walton died in
a car crash on his way to a coin show in 1962, appraisers sur-
prisingly declared his nickel a fake. They marked it "no value,"
returned it to the disappointed family, and the coin stayed hidden in a strongbox on the floor of a closet.

Eventually Walton's nephew, Ryan Givens, inherited
the nickel. Even though it had been dismissed as a counter-
feit, something told him that his uncle was right. In 2003 the

other four 1913 Liberty Head nickels went on display, and a million-dollar prize was offered to anyone who could produce the fifth. Givens submitted his coin for evaluation once more. After hours of comparing and contrasting against the other four nickels, six expert appraisers announced that Walton's coin was *the real deal*.[1]

I just read in the news that Givens sold the nickel for $3.1 million — incidentally, a hundred years after it was originally minted. Imagine that! A coin worth more than $3 million collecting dust in the back corner of a closet for decades and decades because it seemed worthless, even to expert eyes.[2]

It's easy to think, *How could Walton's family possess such a treasure and not even know it?* But the truth is that we ourselves possess a treasure of far greater value than the 1913 Liberty Head nickel. And it's not shoved away in the bottom of a closet; we walk around with it every day. It's the mystery Paul was referring to when he wrote the words, "Christ in you, the hope of glory."[3]

When we are saved, God "recreates" our spirit in that same eternal newness of life. In Ezekiel God says that he gives us a new spirit.[4] This new birth brings about a radical and instantaneous alteration in the core of our being. On the inside we have a new, life-giving nature that is eternal and incorruptible.[5] We are still us, but we are new. We live in the same world but experience it in a fresh way. Paul describes this spiritual phenomenon this way: "If anyone is in Christ, the new creation has come: The old has gone, the new is here!"[6]

The power of Christ is in us, but like Walton's nickel we can't stash it away. We have to dust it off and let it shine. It's the position/function thing we talked about before. The more fulfilled we are *in* Jesus, the more we desire to fulfill our function *for* Jesus. God's priorities become our priorities, including how we act.

It's important—even vital—to say at the outset that seeking after righteousness is not something we can do just by trying hard. We don't get there on our own steam. It's something God does through us as his Spirit comes to live in us—filling us and influencing every part of our nature. But that doesn't mean it's easy.

UNDERSTANDING (AND MISUNDERSTANDING) THE TREASURE

Some of us go wrong when we doubt our position in God's family. Others go wrong in the function department—when we misunderstand how we play our new role.

As a new Christian, I was zealous for the things of God. He had rescued me from a life consumed with partying and getting high. I was using those things to cover up the disappointment and pain I was feeling in other areas of my life. But when I was born again, I underwent an instant, radical change on the inside. The rejuvenating life of God filled all those empty, dry places, and I experienced what Jesus promised: "Whoever believes in me, as Scripture has said, rivers of living water will flow from within them."[7]

Once I experienced the life of God, I never wanted to do anything to mess it up, because this new life was a thousand times better than the best experience I ever had in the clubs. I was seeking joy, fulfillment, and true friendship when I went out partying with my friends, but any pleasure I found was short-lived. When I woke up the next day, that momentary rush was over, usually replaced by a massive headache, nausea, and memories of doing things I wished I hadn't done.

Now I was in God's family. With my new life, God gave me the things I was seeking, but they were permanent and powerful—they didn't vanish like a vapor the next day or leave me riddled with regret and remorse. The experience God gave me was pure and lasting. It welled up from the inside. I no longer needed clubs, partying, drugs, or any other temporary feeling of excitement to feel alive. I *was* alive in the truest possible way—in my spirit.

Because of the gratitude and freedom I experienced, I wanted more of God's presence. I wanted to be more like Christ every day. I used to pray for God to give me more of his Spirit, his character, and his love for others. I know God honored my prayers, but I was praying and living as if God had deposited just enough grace within me to nudge me across the line of salvation. I felt like I had to strive and plead with him for everything else. I believed that the better I did, the more God would reward me by giving me more of his power and grace. If I didn't do well—if I gave in to temptation or failed to complete all my spiritual disciplines for the week—God would withhold his blessing, presence, and power from me. Have you ever had the same feeling?

> The problem was that I didn't need to "get more" of God. I just needed to understand the treasure he'd already given me.

It's funny, because that's not at all how my relationship with God started. When I was saved, I had no illusions that it was because of anything I had done. I knew how useless my own efforts were! Yet my hunger for more of God had left me vulnerable to legalism. It was as if Paul was talking to me when he told the Galatians, "Are you so foolish? After beginning by means of the Spirit, are you now trying to finish by means of the flesh?"[8]

My walk with God began solely and completely by his grace, and yet somehow I thought that everything after "the prayer" was based on the sheer force of my own willpower and self-discipline. Every time I felt spiritually empty, lacking in zeal and power, I prayed to "get more" of God, more of his nature, grace, love, and power. The problem was that I didn't need to "get more" of God. I just needed to understand the treasure he'd already given me.

It wasn't until nearly a decade after I was saved that I truly understood the power-of-God treasure that was within me. Paul tells us that we "have this treasure in earthen vessels, that the excellence of the power may be of God and not of us."[9] I was all too familiar with the earthen vessel. I knew every chip, crack, and leak in mine. I thought that the best way to "carry" the power of God was to patch up that old clay pot and make it as strong and efficient as humanly possible. I wanted my vessel to be worthy of the treasure it was carrying. Even with all my good intentions, the point of Paul's statement was totally lost on me. The jar will never be worthy to carry the treasure within it. In fact, the opposite is true—it's the treasure that gives value to the vessel.

When I finally understood what being "born again" really meant, it started a revolution in my spiritual life. I had been hearing Bible teaching for many years. I prayed, read my Bible, and fasted with so much fervency and zeal that most of my friends thought I was a fanatic—and those were my *Christian* friends! All that time spent developing spiritual disciplines was incredibly important in my walk with God. I still practice all of those disciplines today. They are an important part of living the God-first life. The difference is that I now practice them with the revelation of what "Christ in you, the hope of glory" really means.

Understanding this truth didn't change the way God relates to me, but it did dramatically change the way I relate to him, and even the way I relate to myself. Instead of being focused on what I don't have and what I can't do, I focus on my potential in Christ because I know the power of the new life inside me.

I wonder whether you truly understand the treasure that

has been deposited within you. The life of God in you is present and real—it is bursting at the seams to get out. So let it out. Don't leave it stuffed in the closet like Walton's nickel. Our biggest challenge is not "working up" our faith; it's "working out" our faith—"serv[ing] in the new way of the Spirit," as Paul says.[10] We don't have to keep begging God for more; we just need to cooperate with him to release the power and fruit of the Holy Spirit that is already present inside of us.

A NEW WAY OF DOING LIFE

What does it mean to seek God's righteousness, as Matthew 6:33 instructs? You might have a negative association with the word, especially if you've been on the receiving end of a "self-righteous" attack. But simply put, *righteousness* is God's way of doing things. It refers to the beauty and goodness of who God is and the way that manifests in what he does.

Carry that forward: we act in righteous ways when we reflect his character in our thoughts, decisions, words, and actions. And we "seek" God's righteousness—his right and healthy way of doing things—by reordering our lives around his priorities. God is not working an angle; he just knows what will make us happy and fulfilled.

When you came to faith in Christ, you started a new life. With this new life came the opportunity and the power to exchange your old way of doing things for God's way of doing them. This is at the heart of "seeking righteousness," and it involves a long-term commitment to total personal transformation.

We've talked about how God transforms our spirit. He also transforms our soul—our mind, will, and emotions—the things that make you *you*. But our mind, will, and emotions are also what get us in trouble most often, right? Our appetites, desires, longings, dreams, and fears reside in the soul and are usually the reasons we have a hard time putting God first. As the source of our individuality, the soul is also the root of our independence — the part that fights for its own way, its own plans, and its own purposes. If you do not surrender to the power of the Holy Spirit within you, you will inevitably be driven by your *own* will, caught up in an unending tug of war between your thoughts and emotions, conflicted by your own appetites and desires.

The Bible shows us several types of behaviors that characterize the untransformed life:

greed	selfishness
drunkenness	sexual sin
dishonesty	antagonism
hatred	envy[11]
rage	

Those behaviors characterize us before we decide on the God-first life. Maybe not all of them, but certainly some. Who do you know that doesn't struggle with selfishness? I'm talking about people still breathing. "That is what some of you were," said Paul about the kind of people who act on these impulses. But not anymore. Why? Because "you were washed, you were sanctified, you were justified in the name of the Lord Jesus Christ and by the Spirit of our God."[12]

In another passage Paul says this: "You were taught, with regard to your former way of life, to put off your old self, which is being corrupted by its deceitful desires; to be made new in the attitude of your minds; and to put on the new self, created to be like God in true righteousness and holiness."[13] That's what our new life is supposed to be about. And Paul also tells us what kind of shape that life should take, what kind of behaviors should mark us now:

love	goodness
joy	faithfulness
peace	gentleness
patience	self-control[14]
kindness	

This kind of transformation happens as we choose to put God first, before our passions and desires. As we do that, those around us should notice. In a God-first life, the decisions you make in your heart should manifest themselves in your outer world. Your life should start taking shape in a way that *shows* who is first in a real, concrete way. When you seek God's righteousness, outward evidence will confirm your new inward conviction. Your beliefs will impact and shape the way you live, reflecting your relationship with Christ. This is one of the exciting things about the God-first life—the joy, change, and even miracles that *really* happen when we reflect Christ in our everyday lives.

THE SPIRIT-EMPOWERED LIFE

The traits mentioned above—love, joy, peace, and so on—are called "the fruit of the Holy Spirit." As the Holy Spirit brings us to life, and as we surrender more and more to that new life—discarding the old, self-destructive behavior for the new ways of God's family—it reshapes us over time, and we give evidence of that in new behaviors. But it's important to mention that this is not a one-time project. It's a process. New life in Christ is instant, but it comes with forming, maturing, and cultivating.

The apostle Paul had this process in mind when he admitted to some struggling Christian friends that he was "again in the pains of childbirth *until Christ is formed in you.*"[15] Not to get too literal here, but a baby doesn't happen in a blink. It goes through developmental stages: zygote, blastocyst, embryo, fetus. It's a baby at every step of the way, but there are steps.

The life of Christ in us is the same way. If we're struggling to fully realize our potential in Christ, we can take heart. That's normal. There's an already/not yet quality to it, something explained in Hebrews: "By one sacrifice he has made perfect forever those who are being made holy."[16] Catch that? *Made* and *are being made*. The work of God in our lives is both past and ongoing.

The important thing is to stay connected to the source of our new life. Paul calls it being "filled with the Holy Spirit." We receive the Spirit when we're saved, but staying filled is not a one-time event. It can be, and needs to be, a daily experience, a lifestyle. The apostle compared this to getting drunk. Seriously. "Do not get drunk on wine," he said. "Instead, be filled with the Spirit."[17]

Now, this is not really about drinking. Paul is drawing a contrast between what it requires for a person to become intoxicated and being filled with the Spirit. You can't get drunk on one glass of wine a month, one glass a week, or even one glass a day. You need several glasses in a short time frame to get drunk. (Remember, I used to work in a bar.) Now, if the comparison bothers you, feel free to take that up with Paul when you see him in heaven, but he said the Spirit-filled life is the same way. You can't take a sip now and then. You can't go back to the cup of your first experience with God. You need to pour a new one often.

When we're full of alcohol, drugs, or other excess, we usually overflow with debauchery, revelry, and bad judgment. All the resulting bad effects are a natural by-product of filling up on that stuff. Now use that logic to interpret the positive contrast Paul is making with being filled with the Spirit. The by-products of getting filled up on the Holy Spirit are love, joy, peace, and the rest. We were created for overflow, pouring out into the world what has been poured into us. If we are filled with the Holy Spirit, that's what will flow from us.

We were created for overflow. Whatever you fill up on, that's what's going to flow out of you. If you fill up on all the divisive, negative media, you're going to overflow with depression and negativity. If you fill up on porn, you're going to overflow with lust. If you fill up on the love of money, your life will be all about making a buck and you're going to overflow with greed. But if you fill up on the presence of God, you're going to overflow with the fruit of the Spirit. In time, you'll live more holy on accident than on purpose. But there is purpose involved. We have to decide upfront that we will stay filled with the Holy Spirit, that we will keep coming to the source of our life.

> **We were created for overflow. Whatever you fill up on, that's what's going to flow out of you.**

Have you ever seen a believer fall? I'm talking about someone you maybe looked up to, someone who seemed to have it all together. We all have a war going on inside between our old nature and the new nature that God has implanted in us by his Spirit. The sinful nature wants to do evil; the Spirit wants to honor God. When you see people shipwreck their life, their job, or their marriage, the reason is they let the old nature beat the new. Paul says, "Let the Holy Spirit guide your lives. Then you won't be doing what your sinful nature craves."[18] When we stop letting the Spirit guide us, when we stop being filled, we follow the old desires: anger, lust, jealousy, partying, selfishness, contention. Staying on track means staying filled.

THE POWER OF THE TREASURE

The good news is that being filled is as easy as asking in faith. It needs to be part of our daily prayer. We ask God—and he won't deny us.[19] I add "in faith" because James tells us that "faith by itself, if it is not accompanied by action, is dead."[20] In other words, faith isn't just knowledge. Faith is knowledge plus action. Real faith in human flight is not just knowing about planes. Real faith is getting on board the plane. In the language of the Bible this is "follow[ing] the Spirit's leading in every part of our lives."[21]

Until we make a conscious effort to surrender our will to God's will and yield to the power of the Holy Spirit within us, we will continue to choose, act, and behave just as we did before we got saved. The body will still overwhelm us with its appetites, and the soul will continue to operate in confusion, guided by the thinking and emotions of the old self. In other words, we may have a new spirit on the inside, but on the outside there is no evidence of it—no fruit.

Some people think of the Holy Spirit as a "companion" or a "coach," as if he's Mickey cheering Rocky on from the corner of the boxing ring. The problem with that picture is that the wrong person is in the ring! The Holy Spirit isn't a coach or trainer to be relegated to the sidelines while you duke it out in the ring of life making your own decisions, ducking and weaving on the whims of your own thinking and your own emotions. We are supposed to yield to the Holy Spirit—to *tag out*—so that we are not striving through life's circumstances under our own strength. " 'Not by might nor by power, but by my Spirit,' says the LORD Almighty," as Zechariah tells us.[22]

Putting God first means you are willing to surrender your own will so that God's will (revealed in his Word and confirmed by his Spirit) takes over the reins of your life. Only when you do that will you see transformation occur in your thinking, behaving, and choosing. Strongholds of sin will be broken. Patterns of behavior will be eradicated. Wounds will be healed. And your life will never be the same.

I know that all of these things are easier said than done. Handing all of your habits, choices, past hurts, fears, and worries over to God doesn't happen in an instant. You don't just put them all in a box, tape it up with packing tape, and ship it over to God by overnight delivery. *It's a process.* Even after you think you've given it all over to God, life is still going to throw you curve balls, but you can still walk in freedom. If you learn to trust God and turn the day-to-day circumstances and worries over to him, you will be building a powerful reserve of faith in your soul.

ONE-TIME DECISION VERSUS DAILY CHOICE

Staying filled is a decision. And I mean a decision, not a choice. In our culture we are bombarded by an unending parade of choices, from where to eat, what career to choose, how to exercise, and how to vote (just to name a few)—all driven by a multimedia marketplace focused solely on shaping our consumer preferences. The average person is now acclimated to a daily series of personal choices, all of which are subject to change based on how we feel. And as we know, feelings are likewise subject to change. But we can't approach God as if we're shopping for car insurance.

It's more like a marriage. We decide to love someone, to honor this person, and to serve him or her. We decide that, and then we go about doing it—not perfectly, not flawlessly, but we do it. It's not something we choose: *Do I love my spouse? Do I want what's best for him? Do I care for her?* Yes, yes, and yes. Because you already decided that when you got married, not when you woke up this morning.

The God-first life is not based on something as fickle as a daily choice. It is based on something much more permanent—*decisions.* Decisions are more final, even once and for all. When you decide that you are going to do something, such as following

Christ or choosing your marriage partner, you are establishing something more permanent in nature and determining that it will endure until the end. You experience the God-first life by making *one-time decisions* to establish God's will and ways in your life. These one-time decisions are not to be re-decided daily but are to be *managed* and *protected* for the rest of your life.

This isn't merely defensive. It's an offensive posture against all the false and distracting things in our lives. "Above all else," says the book of Proverbs, "guard your heart, for everything you do flows from it."[23]

> You experience the God-first life by making *one-time decisions* to establish God's will and ways in your life.

When God is first, you will begin to have an awareness of the things that are outside of his will. There may be times when your will conflicts with his will. It is in these times that you have the opportunity to grow the most. When you choose God's way, you will really grow spiritually and experience the rest falling into place as God's complete will for your life comes into alignment. When it comes to engaging God, you get what you put into it. Making right decisions will develop healthy practices, which will eventually lead to a new life of joy and blessing.

By making the overarching decision to live a God-first life as you've been reading, you've probably already made several foundational decisions:

- I will make God's family my primary family.
- I will engage in the community life of the church.
- I will be filled by the Spirit.

And here are four additional decisions for a God-first life:

- I will worship God on my own and with my church family.
- I will spend time with God through prayer and his Word.

- I will give of myself and my means.
- I will experience the freedom, joy, and blessing that God offers.

Similar to deciding to be filled by the Spirit, these decisions are about seeking God's righteousness. According to Matthew 6:33, we're supposed to seek first God's kingdom and righteousness — his way of doing things.

Remember what we said about the word *seeking* in chapter 1; it's about reaching a final determination. These are seven *one-time* decisions. We don't have to keep choosing these values, because we've already chosen them. Now, as you daily manage and protect these core decisions, you will see the patterns of your new family expressed in your new life. God's will and his ways will come into focus, and you will experience the freedom of the abundant life Jesus intended for you.

You need to understand that if you are a Christian, God lives in you. Everywhere you go, and to every person you meet, you are a potential encounter with the life and power of God. Believe it or not, you are now the place where heaven meets earth. You are the temple of the Holy Spirit — a place where the miraculous can happen! Christ is in us. He is the hope of glory, not just to us, but to the people God has entrusted to our sphere of influence. As he is, so are we in this world.

I want to encourage you today. Don't wait for God to change you. He has already done it — you are already changed! You have the treasure with you right now. The power of the Holy Spirit is present within you in complete fullness, but you won't experience it as long as you approach it causally. You are empowered by God, but all that life-changing power will stay unused if you don't respond to God in faith.

SPACE FOR THE SOUL TO BREATHE

Leave Your Problems behind and Enter into God's Presence

Better is one day in your courts than a thousand elsewhere.

Psalm 84:10

I'm originally from Louisiana. This is the land of bayous, quicksand, and swamps. If you try to go through these muddy places, you have to have the right footgear or vehicle to move through. Anyone who has ever gone *mud slingin'* or *mud boggin'* can tell you that you don't head in unless you know you can make it out. You need a big truck with big tires and some serious four-wheel drive. Otherwise, you *will* get stuck.

Let's face it—our world can feel like a swamp sometimes. You might be knee-deep in financial trouble, marriage problems, or other concerns. You might feel like you are trying to navigate life through a muddy mess, but you're driving a Nissan Leaf. Nothing against the Leaf. I like golf carts just fine. But it won't get you through the swamp.

There is a vehicle that cannot be slowed down by the

"mud" of this world, and that vehicle is worship. There is a high ground in God where only worship can take you. There is a connection, a *lifeline*, that is established between you and God during worship, and it is during the connection of worship that God pulls us out of the mud and into his presence. "He lifted me out of the slimy pit, out of the mud and mire; he set my feet on a rock and gave me a firm place to stand," David says in the Psalms. "He put a new song in my mouth, a hymn of praise to our God. Many will see and fear the LORD and put their trust in him."[1]

God can pull us out of a horrible pit. And even though life is constantly slinging mud on us and we get bogged down by the challenges, distractions, and obligations of life, God does not want you stuck in a rut. He wants you to know that he will always see you through.

Peter tells us that God "has given us everything we need for a godly life."[2] In other words, God has equipped us with divine resources that, if we understand their power and how to deploy them, will help us avoid getting stuck in the mud of our circumstances. Ready access to God through worship is one of the most powerful resources we've been given. Nothing has a more immediate impact on us and our circumstances than the presence of God. Worship is absolutely necessary for living life God's way and putting him up high above all else in our lives.

EXPERIENCING GOD

Before I decided to make God first, I felt church and God were disconnected. I don't mean to sound critical, but I found church dull as chalk, even though I knew God couldn't be that. How could God be boring? I also saw church as a waste of time. The pastor talked about things that didn't much apply in my life, or at least they didn't seem to. On the upside, the people in my church weren't judgmental per se, but I did know plenty of folks who had experienced those disapproving eyes and sideways glances as they eased into a pew. Who doesn't?

A survey conducted by the Barna Group found a sizeable percentage of young Christians have found church "boring" and basically irrelevant to their life. The real shock was how many agreed with the statement, "God seems missing from my experience of church."[3] No wonder it feels boring and irrelevant.

I wonder what would happen if we realized that one of the purposes of corporate worship is to experience God. God has designed worship as the vehicle for experiencing his presence. The bad news is that many churches seem to view worship as singing a song and making some declarations about God. Sure, that's part of it. But worship is not singing, and we shouldn't confuse one for the other.

The goal of worship is to (1) engage, (2) encounter, and (3) experience the presence of the everlasting God. That's what people are looking for; that's what they're searching for. Here's the good news—the amazing, mind-boggling, earth-shaking news. People are seeking to experience God, and that's just what God wants to give them. God wants us to experience him too. We can see this simple truth about worship illustrated in an encounter between Jesus and an unlikely woman.

WHEN YOU'RE BROKENHEARTED

In John 4, Jesus taught his first lesson on worship. He didn't teach that lesson to his disciples. He taught it to an adulterous Samaritan woman—which is really surprising. Back in that day she would have been *below* the bottom rung of the social ladder. He met her at a well, and Jesus sat and waited for this divine appointment.

The woman arrived to draw water, and Jesus asked her for a drink. This caught her off guard. She could tell Jesus was a Jew, and Jews didn't have anything to do with Samaritans. Why? The Samaritans were the descendants of Jews who had inter-married with pagan colonists brought to the region by Assyrian conquerors centuries earlier; they had created their own place of worship on Mount Gerizim instead of the temple in Jerusalem. That was a no-no. Prejudice against Samaritans was not only permitted by first-century Jews; it was expected. Disdain for the Samaritans showed one's devotion to the purity of the tradition of Moses. For a Jew like Jesus to talk with this Samaritan was a shock, even more so since he asked her for a drink of water.

But that was only the first of three strikes against the woman at the well. The next is simply that she *was* a woman. This was long before women's liberation and well before Southern man-ners. In the culture at that time, being a woman made you inferior. Women were not granted the same access to worship in the temple courts afforded men. Yet Jesus' first message on worship—hang on, it's coming—was to a woman.

The third strike was her adultery. She had already had five husbands, and at the point Jesus met her, she was living with a man to whom she wasn't married. Even though we don't know the story of her life and how all those relationships ended and started, there is one thing we can be sure of: this was a broken woman.

We shouldn't find it surprising that the words "broken," "oppressed," and "despised" describe Jesus' student of worship. People like her are the reason Jesus came. When Jesus launched his ministry with this mission statement, he left no uncertainty about his purpose:

The Spirit of the Lord is on me,
    because he has anointed me
    to proclaim good news to the poor.
He has sent me to proclaim freedom for the prisoners
    and recovery of sight for the blind,

to set the oppressed free,
to proclaim the year of the Lord's favor.[4]

In the language of our day, we would say that the Samaritan woman was the poster child of the Messiah campaign. She represented every wrong he came to set right.

Making this encounter even more interesting, the woman was the one who brought up worship, not Jesus. She wanted to know what true worship was. She wanted to know if, when, and how she could experience the presence of God. The religious debates of the day were about form and access: Where is the right place to worship God? Who is allowed into his presence? More importantly, who is *not* allowed into his presence? I have a feeling the Samaritan woman would have put herself in the "not allowed" category. And yet here was this Jewish rabbi talking to her about worship, listening to her as if her opinions really mattered.

He started by talking about living water. More than physically thirsty, she was spiritually thirsty—and Jesus knew it. Before she could get over the shock that this Jewish man was asking her for water, Jesus gave her another shock: "If you knew the gift of God and who it is that asks you for a drink, you would have asked him and he would have given you living water," he said. "Indeed, the water I give [to a person] will become in [that person] a spring of water welling up to eternal life."[5] When

> In true worship, your heart will never go thirsty again.

Jesus referred to "living water," he was talking about quenching the desire of the human heart that only worship can bring. In true worship, your heart will never go thirsty again.

Jesus moved the Samaritan woman over to the allowed category with these words: "A time is coming and has now come when the true worshipers will worship the Father in the Spirit and in truth, for they are the kind of worshipers the Father seeks."[6]

The people who experience worship the way the Father intends are those who worship him "in the Spirit and in truth." The rivers of living water are released in your life through engaging God in worship. That is the practice the Father has ordained this side of heaven. God is not flesh; God is Spirit. So we have to come and worship in Spirit and truth. And every single time, the living water of Christ is going to flow through us.

The fact that Jesus chose to teach the Samaritan woman first of all about worship speaks to the point of worship itself. The *who* here speaks to the *what*. This woman had a hard life and she needed a reprieve. Jesus was there to offer her one.

"AT THAT MOMENT"

The prophet Malachi revealed God's desire to draw all people to himself and allow them full access to his presence in worship. "The nations ... [will worship me] from where the sun rises to where it sets," says God.[7] We can see God drawing all people into worship powerfully foreshadowed in 2 Chronicles. After Solomon built the temple, the priests and all the people gathered to dedicate it to the Lord:

> The priests then withdrew from the Holy Place. All the priests who were there had consecrated themselves, regardless of their divisions. All the Levites who were musicians—Asaph, Heman, Jeduthun and their sons and relatives—stood on the east side of the altar, dressed in fine linen and playing cymbals, harps and lyres. They were accompanied by 120 priests sounding trumpets. The trumpeters and musicians joined in unison to give praise and thanks to the LORD. Accompanied by trumpets, cymbals and other instruments, the singers raised their voices in praise to the LORD and sang:
>
> "He is good;
>   his love endures forever."[8]

Imagine this scene. The Levites are bringing the ark, containing the very presence of God, into the temple, and all of the priests are gathered there. Some of these priests are playing instruments—trumpets, lyres, cymbals, and harps—and they begin to sing to the Lord. Then everybody begins to sing in unison. They begin to declare about God: "He is good; his love endures forever."

Does this sound like something you are familiar with? This worship format is how most churches do it today. We don't have priests and Levites, but we have people who are called and anointed to lead others in worship. They come into the house of God every weekend, and they sing and play instruments, but they're not just singing *about* God. They're not putting on a concert or engaging you in a sing-along. That is not what worship is all about. Those singers and musicians deploy their gifts for the pure and holy purpose of ushering you into the presence of God. For the priests and Levites in the temple, all of the music and singing was a means to an end. It was all leading up to one moment—the moment of experiencing the presence of God.

The Scriptures go on to say, "At that moment a thick cloud filled the Temple of the LORD. The priests could not continue their service because of the cloud."[9] We know that when God stirs, all flesh must "be still before LORD," as the Bible says.[10] That's what happens when the glory of God's presence fills the temple.

The Old Testament priests and Levites were following a legal contract, or covenant, that allowed them to have access to God only if they were present in a temple building. But under the *new* covenant, established by Jesus on the cross, your *body* is now the temple of the Lord, as Christ lives in you.[11] Worship is no longer restricted to a physical location or building. You have the very presence of God, the "Holies of Holies," inside you. You *are* the temple.

There are a lot of things in the Christian life that are a process. Growth is a process. Sometimes deliverance and freedom are a process. But there's one practice, this side of heaven, where processes can be temporarily bypassed, and you can have a reprieve from the struggles of the flesh and the pain of this world. *Worship.* Every Christian is invited before the throne of God. It doesn't matter how long you've been a believer, how much progress you've made in the Holy Spirit, how spiritual you think you are (or aren't). You're invited. Whatever it is that weighs you down, sets you back, or keeps you up at night, set it down and come.

The most powerful reality of worship is that the more we press into God, the more we pull away from our flesh. I've never seen people who are engaged in the presence of God lose their temper. I've never seen anybody experiencing the presence of God while simultaneously looking at inappropriate images on the Internet or seething in unforgiveness toward a friend. I've never seen people consumed with worry, anxiety, depression, or despair when they are in the presence of God. All of this grows still before the throne of God.

When Lexie was six months pregnant with her first child, she told me that she suffered through a lengthy period of restlessness. She was totally exhausted but could not drift off to sleep. She was scared, fatigued, frustrated, and growing hopeless. Who wouldn't be? Worship was the answer. God led Lexie to pour her heart out in worship, and it worked. She began to feel peace and was soon experiencing deep and satisfying sleep. "By positioning myself in the presence of the Almighty through worship, darkness had to flee," she told me. "It wasn't just a temporary victory either. I now constantly use worship to draw near to God and exalt him, and as a powerful weapon against my adversary. God truly does inhabit the praises of his people."

Worship is a momentary break from our own conflicted flesh and the challenges of this world. It's the only time this side of heaven in this life that you will get relief from your flesh—your sinful desires and habits. In heaven, there will be no more tears, no more pain, and no more temptation. What you experience during worship on this side of eternity is merely a glimpse into what we will all experience with our God when we can dwell with him in heaven. It's just a single drop in an ocean of oceans. But just one drop of God's living water can satisfy the soul.

When you engage God in worship, at that moment his presence fills your temple and your flesh grows still. The pain you're experiencing, the sin, the temptation, the mud that life slings at you—at that moment, those things can't get the edge on you. There's no place for them because his presence fills your temple.

It will just be for that moment, but at that moment, God says, *I want to give you a break. You've been out there on the battlefield. You've been out there in the mud. You've been getting dirt slung on you all week. But when you come into my presence, you're my son; you're my daughter. I love you. And at this moment, I want you to get a reprieve. No flesh will be able to stand in my presence.*

Worship is an at-that-moment experience. It's a gift from God, and it's available to every believer.

THE VALLEY OF BLESSING

Besides giving us relief from our flesh, worship affords us an opportunity to face down the enemies that come against us in life. More accurately, it puts us in a position of trust and surrender to God as we let him fight on our behalf.

Nothing highlights this more than the story of King Jehoshaphat. He was one of a handful of righteous kings of Judah, but he had enemies. When he started getting reports that a massive force was on the march against him and his people, he prayed, "We have no power to face this vast army that is attacking us. We do not know what to do, but our eyes are on you." How often are we in the same situation—facing impossible odds? The amazing thing is what God said in response: "The battle is not yours, but God's."[12]

The next day, Judah's army marched out to meet the enemy. But King Jehoshaphat did not place his fiercest men at the head of the army, his crack troops and commandos. No, if you can believe it, he sent the choir first. "Jehoshaphat appointed men to sing to the LORD and to praise him for the splendor of his holiness as they went out at the head of the army, saying: 'Give thanks to the LORD, for his love endures forever.'"[13]

And here's where everything changed. Instead of attacking Judah, the enemy army divided, and the men started fighting each other. By the time Jehoshaphat's army arrived on the scene, it was all over.

> When the men of Judah came to the place that overlooks the desert and looked toward the vast army, they saw only dead bodies lying on the ground; no one had escaped. So Jehoshaphat and his men went to carry off their plunder, and they found among them a great amount of equipment and clothing and also articles of value—more than they could take away. There was so much plunder that it took three days to collect it.[14]

Worship is a space maker. Jehoshaphat understood the importance of making space for God in the midst of his battle. When he and his men went into battle, everything was against them. They were totally outnumbered. The natural inclination of most kings would be to try to make peace with the enemy. The Bible tells us our real enemy is not a person or a circumstance but spiritual forces that stand against everyone who trusts in Christ.[15] God doesn't want us to make peace with those enemies; he wants to *be our peace* in the presence of our enemies. How? According to the Psalms, God is "enthroned on the praises of Israel."[16] Other translations say that he "inhabits"

Israel's praises — that he dwells with them. God is with us. So Jehoshaphat sent singers, and God fought the battle while the people praised him.

We are just like Jehoshaphat. Every week we find ourselves totally outnumbered. We've got everything going against us in our relationship with God. We've got our own flesh — that's bad enough. How often have you said or heard the phrase "I am my own worst enemy"? But on top of that, we've got temptation, discouragement, disappointment, and frustration. And that's not all.

On top of all that, we've got the devil. His goal is to steal, kill, and destroy everything good in your life. And he does it without an ounce of pity or remorse — only relentless opposition.

The only way to stand up to that kind of battle is to send out the singers. The only way to beat those odds is to worship, to make a space of praise for God to inhabit. At that moment, no enemy will be able to stand. At that moment, your flesh can't win. Like in Jehoshaphat's story, our enemies are defeated in worship. God changes our perspective. Instead of seeing an army standing against us, suddenly — in a moment — we are victorious.

After the Lord fought the battle for Jehoshaphat, "on the fourth day they gathered in the Valley of Blessing, which got its name that day because the people praised and thanked the LORD there. It is still called the Valley of Blessing today."[17] The Lord fought the battle, but the people got the blessing. They did what they could do — they worshiped him and praised him. And then he did what only he could do — he defeated the enemy when they did not have any hope. The place of battle became a valley of blessing, and the outcome hinged on the worship of the people.

Every week there is battle waiting for you, but a Valley of

Blessing is waiting for you too. Every week, there is a place where praise is going up to God. If you will come to that Valley of Blessing, where the praise is going on, God will inhabit your praises. He'll fight your battles for you, and you'll be able to pick up spiritual blessings like peace and joy—things that money cannot buy.

God wants you to become a worshiper and to understand the power of worship. You can worship in your car or at your house. In fact, we should worship God all the time. Worshiping God weekly and consistently keeps our flesh in a weakened state. And while we're not bound to a specific time or physical location to experience the presence of God through worship, there is a special presence and power in corporate worship. This is why it's so important to be faithful in fellowship with other believers, especially in weekend services in the local church.

EXPERIENCING THE PRESENCE OF GOD

Ultimately we need to remember that worship—however we do it—is about (1) *engaging* God with our bodies, which leads to (2) an *encounter* with God in our minds, from which we (3) *experience* God in our souls. What that means is that, above all, we have to worship actively.

You may or may not have experienced the presence of God in such a personal, tangible way. Worship is a spiritual experience, one that takes us to the limits of what words can adequately describe. It's like trying to explain to someone what love feels like—words can only come up short. The best way for you to understand what I am describing is to experience it for yourself.

Even though it is difficult to describe experiencing God, it's actually not difficult to do. There are three steps to experiencing the presence of God in worship, and each of these ways helps lead us toward experiencing God's presence.

1. *Engaging God with your strength*, or your body. Jesus said, "Love the Lord your God with all your heart and with all your soul and with all your strength and with all your mind."[18] In the act of worship, experiencing the love of God in your heart involves the engagement of your strength, mind, and soul.

We do this as an act of our will and not as our emotions or feelings dictate. When you come to the worship service, you may not feel like worshiping. Maybe it hasn't been the best week for you. You're sleepy, or you're busy, worried, or distracted. The normal response during times like these is to let our feelings dictate how we worship. You might not feel like clapping, but guess what? You can clap when you don't feel like it. You might not feel like singing, but guess what? You can sing without feeling like it too! Start to engage God. Make a move. The Psalms say, "Clap your hands, all you nations; shout to God with cries of joy.... Sing praises to God, sing praises."[19] All these things involve the initiation of our strength. We're not waiting for something to happen.

I frequently hear people say, *I want my worship to be genuine and sincere. I don't want to fake it. God wants me to be authentic with him.* To tell you the truth, there are many mornings I arrive at church and don't feel like worshiping. You might be surprised to find out how many pastors feel that way. When I walk into church, I am usually thinking about my message, special items that have to take place in the service, or meetings I have afterward. If I drive up and find a traffic jam in the parking lot or the air conditioning is broken in my car, worshiping is the last thing on my mind.

I'm thankful I made the decision to be a worshiper long before God ever called me to be a pastor. No matter how I feel, I know that I am going to worship God. The funny thing is that when I *choose* to worship God, all of the things that made me feel like not worshiping in the first place don't seem that important anymore. Putting God first, before my feelings, turns a simple move toward God into authentic worship.

2. *Encounter God with your mind.* What starts with the physical now moves to the mind. We're transformed by the renewing of our minds. When you sing songs that declare truth about God—his love, faithfulness, goodness, and glory—it changes how you see your circumstances. The Bible describes this as "magnifying the Lord." When we magnify something, we make it fill more of our focus, take more of our attention, occupy more of our mind. Suddenly, we have a way of judging the importance of everything in our lives based on how they compare to the most important thing in our lives.

When we magnify God through worship, in that moment he is the most important thing in our lives. He is first. And in comparison to his greatness, our problems don't seem so big. When we bring him into focus, it puts everything else in perspective. "Since, then, you have been raised with Christ, set your hearts on things above, where Christ is, seated at the right hand of God. Set your minds on things above, not on earthly things."[20]

Encountering God with our minds will mean focusing on not just the music of the songs but also the words. There's always a message in the music. When we worship, we set our minds on the lyrics and what they say about Christ and who we are in him.

As we encounter God in our minds, we will also feel his presence through our emotions. The way we participate in worship should never take the focus off God and put it on ourselves. At the same time, God made you in his image. He gave you emotions. Somehow people have come to think that worship that expresses emotion is abnormal. I'm sorry, but that's weird. Why wouldn't normal worship express some sort of emotion, maybe all sorts of emotions?

If you're passionate about something, you're going to be emotional about it. We get emotional every day about all kinds of things. Nobody has to tell us to cheer when our team scores or tear up when our kids do something adorable. Nobody has to tell you to laugh when something funny happens or to scream when you are going down the first huge slope of a roller coaster. Emotions are a natural, normal response to life. Yet when it comes to what's eternal, all of a sudden we get cynical and distrustful about the role our emotions play. We try to make the faith life all about beliefs and lifestyles. But it's also about an experience, and experiences lead to emotions.

All the Old Testament accounts of worship are festive and lively. It's like a party. It's Miriam playing the tambourine, the priests shouting, and David dancing. It's the presence of God filling the temple. It's the prodigal son coming home. It's Jesus going to the house of sinners. It's someone repenting and all of heaven rejoicing. It's a celebration!

Then, when you start thanking God, when you focus your mind on him, that leads to the final step.

3. *Experiencing God in your soul.* Experiencing God is the best part of worship. It's like nothing else on earth. If you have never experienced the presence of God, then you probably thought I was exaggerating when you read that sentence. Maybe you are running down a list of experiences in your head and thinking there's no way experiencing God could compare with *that*. But if you have experienced the presence of God, you know just what I'm talking about. Your response to that statement was different. You have tasted the living water, and you know nothing can compare to it. This is where God wants to take us—the at-that-moment experience, where nothing compares and the weight of the world lessens.

The Psalms describe worship in experiential terms. "Taste and see that the LORD is good" is one of my favorites.[21] And another: "As the deer pants for streams of water, so my soul pants for you, my God. My soul thirsts for God, for the living God. When can I go and meet with God?"[22] There is a component of our spirituality that is supposed to be experiential, and that component is worship. However, even after we have engaged worship with our strength and encountered God with our minds, we still have to yield to experiencing him.

The third chapter of Revelation shows how Jesus invites us to experience him. It's important to know that in this section of Revelation, Jesus was not speaking to the unsaved but to the saved. He is not asking the unsaved to be saved, but rather he is inviting the saved to experience him at a deeper level. He says, "Here I am! I stand at the door and knock. If anyone hears my voice and opens the door, I will come in and eat with that person, and they with me."[23]

The Lord inhabits the praises of his people. Now he's standing at the door of your heart, and he's saying, *Will you go ahead and abandon yourself to me? Will you just let me in?* And at that moment of abandonment and surrender you experience the presence of God. That's where you get a reprieve from the world, and God pulls back the veil for a moment and gives you a little taste of heaven. He says, *I know it's been tough. Listen, I love you. You're going to be with me forever one day.*

As I said above, worship is a spiritual experience. The best way for you to understand what I am describing is to experience it for yourself. Commit to being a sincere worshiper, in Spirit and in truth. Remember—engage, encounter, and experience. Your worship of God will never be the same.

YOU'VE GOT TO FEED YOURSELF

Cultivate Your Relationship with God through Personal Devotions

Man shall not live on bread alone, but on every word that comes from the mouth of God.

Matthew 4:4

What is it about becoming a first-time parent that causes adults to start babbling like babies? Like most new parents, Kerri and I did. It didn't take long before we had our own baby jargon—not to mention all the nicknames for nearly every item in the nursery. Baby bottles were, for example, "baba's." Pacifiers were called "paci's."

Our first daughter especially loved her baba and paci. The only way to get Kaylan to sleep was to load her down with a full bottle and about twenty paci's, spread around her head like a halo. No matter how hard she resisted sleep, as soon as she got that baba in one hand and a paci in the other, those eyelids started to droop. One by one, she would try out the paci's, looking for the perfect fit. As soon as she found it, she was out like a light.

Until the baba was dry. If Kaylan didn't receive a refill soon after her bottle was empty, the Baba Meltdown would commence. It always followed a specific and predictable pattern. First came the slurping sound of the bottle being drained, followed by the first faint chirp: "Baba." The clock started here.

After about ten seconds, the request was repeated with a little more force and urgency. "Ba-ba." You had until the twenty-second mark, at which point the final threat was issued. If there were no response, Kaylan would clutch the empty baba and raise it above her head, chanting with rising volume and intensity, "Ba-BA! Ba-BA! Ba-BA!" Without immediate action, Operation Baba Meltdown would go code red. Wailing would ensue, and the empty baba would come humming through the air like the stone from David's sling, with your head the intended target.

Thank goodness Kaylan is sixteen now and capable of feeding herself. How about you? Part of maturing spiritually is learning how to feed yourself, and learning to do it frequently. As an adult, if you waited for others to feed you, you'd probably starve. Likewise, if you only ate one meal a week, you'd never have the physical energy to meet the needs of your life. You'd shrivel up and die. Spiritually, it is the same way. Although faithfully attending weekend services plays a vital role in feeding and sustaining your spiritual life, you can't just live Sunday to Sunday, hoping to get enough from a few hours at church.

A huge part of putting God first—one that pays off big time—is taking the responsibility to pray and to study God's Word for yourself throughout the week. Getting to know him better is how you know how to change your life so you can start living according to his ways. You will be seeking his thoughts, his kingdom, his righteousness before all else.

DEVOTED TO GOD SEVEN DAYS A WEEK

Too many people have a "feed me" approach to spiritual growth. They come to church on Sunday with their imaginary spiritual babas raised in the air.

"Everybody better treat me right and smile at me," they

practically threaten. "And, Preacher, you better bring the Word, and it better be a great message, and you better have a bunch of Scriptures to back it up, and it better be funny, and you better have some memorable illustrations, and it better not be too long or ... or ... or ... *waaahhh!*" It's like they're having their own Baba Meltdown.

Here's the reality. No matter how good the preaching is at your church, it's only part of what you need each week. Your pastor can't be responsible to feed you all you require once a week, and there's no way you'll survive spiritually on just one meal. It's like we said in chapter 5 about being filled with the Spirit. It's a daily thing, not something we do every now and then.

And let's not trick ourselves. We need more than sermons. Jesus didn't redeem our lives on the cross so we could listen to someone talk at us for forty-five minutes a week. As I said in chapters 3 and 4, you can't fully live the Christian life unless you do so in and with the local church. That's not saying that you can't be a Christian, that you can't have faith, or that you can't be saved. But this isn't about finding the lowest common denominator. Jesus redeemed us for a relationship.

We can have a great experience on Sunday for a while, but our spiritual life will shrivel if we're not cultivating our relationship with Jesus all week. Besides taking time to worship during the week, that means taking time to pray and meditate on God's Word. We call this time of prayer and study *devotions*.

In my experience, few people understand that to get the most out of the Word on Sunday, you've got to get more of the Word Monday through Saturday. The more you pray and read the Scriptures, the better you will understand them. And hear me: the more you pray and read the Scriptures, the better you will understand Jesus. Why? You grow to know those with whom you spend your time. We'll see how we do that in both prayer and Bible study. Let's start with prayer.

TALKING WITH GOD

Even in Christian circles, I've learned that prayer can seem to be a mystery to people. Some things you pray for happen; some things you pray for don't happen; some things you never pray for happen. There are a lot of often-humorous misconceptions about prayer and approaching God. Remember Chevy Chase's prayer when Aunt Edna died in *National Lampoon's Vacation*?

> Okay, bow your heads. Bow your heads. Oh, God, ease our suffering in this, our moment of great despair. Yea, admit this good and decent woman into thine arms and the flock in thine heavenly area up there.... And yea, though the Hindus speak of Karma, I implore you, give her—give her a break....

Apparently some of us don't realize it's a joke. I've actually heard similar prayers, and you probably have too. It's as if we think God only speaks King James English. Not so. Let's be clear about this: prayer is about relationship. There's nothing wrong with using elevated words. Different situations require different language; a husband, for instance, speaks to his wife at the grocery store differently than he does on the beach at sunset. But either way, it should be genuine because it's about connection.

Christ's ministry was about restoring our relationship with God. The only way to be a healthy Christian is to commune with God daily through prayer. Every person who has ever been effective in service for God has developed a consistent prayer life. If we're unsure about how to approach God, that's normal. Thankfully, Jesus himself teaches us in the words of the Lord's Prayer:

> Our Father in heaven,
> hallowed be your name,
> your kingdom come,
> your will be done,

on earth as it is in heaven.
Give us today our daily bread.
And forgive us our debts,
    as we also have forgiven our debtors.
And lead us not into temptation,
    but deliver us from the evil one.
For yours is the kingdom and the power
and the glory forever. Amen.[1]

We can pray these simple words by themselves or use them as the beams and studs to construct our own prayers. First, we can break down each petition, notice its purpose, and use the pattern to find a new way to apply it:

PETITION	TYPE	APPLICATION
Our Father in heaven, hallowed be your name.	Praise	We begin by expressing love to God.
Your kingdom come, your will be done, on earth as it is in heaven.	Purpose	We commit ourselves to doing God's will.
Give us this day our daily bread.	Provision	We ask God to provide our daily needs.
Forgive us our debts …	Pardon	We ask God to forgive our sins.
… as we also have forgiven our debtors.	People	We pray for others.
And lead us not into temptation, but deliver us from the evil one.	Protection	We ask for spiritual protection.
For yours is the kingdom and the power and the glory forever. Amen.[2]	Praise	We close by expressing love and honor to God.

As you offer your own prayer, keep that pattern in mind: praise, purpose, provision, pardon, people, protection, and then back to praise.

Next, here's another way to pray this prayer. Focus on the three things God makes new in our lives when we seek his kingdom. The first part of the prayer is about our family. "Our Father in heaven, hallowed be your name, your kingdom come, your will be done, on earth as it is in heaven." The middle part of the prayer covers our new life of dependence on and surrender to God. "Give us today our daily bread." We turn to God for our needs and stop striving on our own. The third part deals with our new freedom in Christ. "And forgive us our debts, as we also have forgiven our debtors. And lead us not into temptation, but deliver us from the evil one."

I've used the Lord's Prayer in my regular devotion time as a guide to putting God first in my life for years now. It's simple, covering all my needs, and I learned from the Teacher himself.

I start at the start. "Our Father, hallowed be thy name." I begin thanking God for his goodness and greatness. Thankfulness is a big part of that praise in the beginning. It's important for us to be reminded that God is our Father and what a blessing it is to belong to his family.

Prayer starts with an attitude of thankfulness. Do not start with confessing your sins. Notice in the Lord's Prayer that forgiveness is the fourth thing. This is important. When we pray, "Forgive us our sins as we forgive those who sin against us," it's from a relational and fellowship standpoint with God; it's not about losing our salvation or position in God's family.

I pray that his kingdom come and his will be done. This ties back to Matthew 6:33 and the God-first life. This petition reaffirms my commitment to a God-first life that will bring him glory. I pray his will in and through me, my family, and the church. God's will is accomplished once again by seeking him and his righteousness first.

When I move to asking God for my daily bread, I ask him to be the source of all of my needs and thank him for providing me everything I require to accomplish his purpose. And as a parent, I'll especially focus on what my kids need.

Now, finally, I get to forgiveness. I cannot overstate how important it is to keep things in the priority God established. God doesn't want us obsessing on our sins. Placing this fourth gives us a check—*Have I offended God? How have I treated people?*—but it avoids turning my sin into the whole story. I ask forgiveness and grace to overcome temptation.

Next I ask about having that same sort of forgiveness toward others—"as we also have forgiven our debtors." This part of the Lord's Prayer gives me a self-check and helps me with an attitude of forgiveness toward others. This part of the prayer reminds us where we came from. We forgive others not because they deserve it; we forgive others because of Jesus. God is first in my life, and so I offer to others the same thing he offers me.

"And lead us not into temptation." I really believe that praying this prayer over the years has protected me so much. We know that plans and schemes of the enemy. Evil is at work in the world. By praying this we acknowledge God is our shelter and confess our faith that he will guide and protect us.

Then I go back to thanksgiving, praying, "Yours is the kingdom and the power and the glory forever." Thanksgiving is such a powerful fruit of my devotional time. This way of approaching the Lord's Prayer is simple, but it works for me.

I'm not saying there aren't other ways to pray. I'm not saying you have to do it this way. There are as many prayers as there are people. "Lord, have mercy" is the most repeated prayer in the Bible.[3] Sometimes that's the only thing that makes sense to pray. And when we can't find the words, when we don't know what to ask, we know from the Bible that the Spirit prays in us. "The Spirit himself intercedes for us through wordless groans," says Paul. "And he who searches our hearts knows the mind of the Spirit, because the Spirit intercedes for God's people in accordance with the will of God."[4] The main thing is that we're genuine and sincerely seeking a deeper relationship with Jesus.

However we do it, establishing a consistent, daily time of personal prayer will be a catalyst for God's power and provision in your life. For most people, first thing in the morning is best. God's mercies are "new every morning."[5] "It is good to praise the LORD," according to the Psalms, "proclaiming your love in the morning."[6] Others may pull away for some time during their lunch hour or at the end of the day. Some find it effective to utilize all those times. Whenever you do it, just do it. We meet Jesus in prayer—don't miss the appointment.

This is part of what the Bible is talking about when the apostle Paul encourages us to "pray continually."[7] That doesn't mean praying nonstop, twenty-four hours a day; that's mentally and physically impossible. What it does mean is you develop a rhythm in prayer.

It's not just something you do in one season and not in another. Don't save it all for traffic court or a bad day at the job. It's like any other activity we continually do: eating, working, sleeping, whatever. Walking and talking with Jesus should be part of our daily rhythm.

WHY WE CAN'T SEE JESUS

On the morning of the resurrection, Jesus traveled with two of his disciples incognito. These two guys were on their way back from the Passover feast in Jerusalem to their home in a town called Emmaus. As they walked along, talking about everything that had happened over the past few days—Judas's betrayal, the trial, the crucifixion, the mysteriously empty tomb—Jesus came along and began walking with them. Somehow they didn't realize it was him, like he was in disguise.[8]

Unrecognized, Jesus jumped right into the conversation without telling them who he was. He talked about Scriptures—the Law, the Prophets, and the Psalms—and showed them how all the writings of the Old Testament pointed to him, even though they had no idea it was him. By the time they reached the house, these two were so captivated by Jesus' teaching that they begged him not to leave and offered him dinner and a room for the night. When they sat down to eat, Jesus broke bread. Suddenly the lights came on for the two disciples. In that moment they recognized who he was.[9]

Imagine how they must have felt to realize that it was Jesus all along, walking with them on a seven-mile journey, practically telling them his whole life story in the prophecies of the Scripture, and yet they didn't recognize who he was until they were sitting down to dinner.

Do you wonder how those two men could have been with Jesus and not recognized him for all that time? The road to Emmaus is just one of several instances where the same thing happened. Outside the tomb, Mary Magdalene thought Jesus was a gardener, there to tend the grounds.[10] The disciples who were out in the boat fishing thought he was just another guy cooking breakfast on the shore.[11] All of these people were followers of Jesus. They had heard him teach and seen him do miracles. They were devastated by his death and beside themselves with grief. You would think that the minute they saw him their faces would light up at the sight. If seeing is believing, then these people should have been jumping for joy.

So, is seeing really believing? By looking at the way people responded to Jesus after the resurrection, the answer seems to be no. In all of these instances, Jesus' identity was revealed, not when they saw him, but when he spoke to them. Jesus revealed himself through his words—through *the Word*.

In the new kingdom, believing comes not by seeing but by

hearing the word of God.[12] It wasn't until after Jesus opened the Scriptures to the disciples on the road to Emmaus that their eyes were opened and they recognized him for who he was. The disciples said their spirits burned within them as he talked with them. Mary recognized Jesus when he spoke to her. The disciples who were out in the boat fishing recognized Jesus when he called out to them. When Jesus spoke, each of them became more aware of his presence.

This should encourage us. It means that there are no special advantages in the kingdom, no spiritual caste system.[13] It's not like some people can know Jesus better than others, not even because they walked with him. We all meet Jesus in the same place — the Word.

The reality is that we are never alone in life because God promises never to leave us or forsake us. However, we may not be aware of his presence if, when we are seeking him, we do not know what to look for. The same things that kept the disciples from recognizing Jesus on the road to Emmaus keep us from recognizing him today.

"How foolish you are," Jesus told the two on the Emmaus road, "and how slow to believe all that the prophets have spoken!"[14]

Those are strong words. *Jesus called them foolish.* He wasn't saying that they were stupid but that their understanding was immature. The disciples' knowledge of Scripture was simply not deep enough for them to *see God* in the events that had taken place in Jerusalem. They totally missed the fact that Jesus' trial and crucifixion, the very things that were discouraging them and causing them to doubt, affirmed his identity as the Messiah. If we don't open the Scriptures for ourselves, we won't be able to see Jesus for who he is.

Just as worship leads us to a moment where we experience the presence of God, studying the Scriptures leads us to a moment where we have a revelation of Christ. In that moment—the moment when we see Jesus revealed—everything can turn around. As soon as Jesus opened the word to the disciples, their eyes were opened to him.

Their vision went from cloudy to clear.

Their despair turned to joy.

Their weakness turned to strength.

Their hope was renewed.

Not only that, but they had a change of direction. Though they had trudged all the way home to Emmaus and were bone tired, they turned around immediately and headed straight back to Jerusalem.

The name Jerusalem means "Foundation of Peace." Are you living in obscurity when it comes to understanding who you are in Christ? Are you foggy about your relationship with God, constantly wavering between passion for God and the pull of the world? If you want to get out of obscurity and back to peace, you have to make the decision to open the Scriptures on a daily basis.

SLOW TO BELIEVE

There's another thing that stands out in this story of Emmaus. Notice that Jesus also called the two disciples "slow to believe." Sometimes we can't get the breakthroughs in life we need, not because we lack knowledge, or even because our understanding is immature. Sometimes the problem is that we are seeking God's kingdom and righteousness in our devotional time, but we are slow to open our hearts and believe what the Scriptures are actually telling us.

I determined long ago that I want to be the kind of person who is quick to believe what God's Word says. And *quick to believe* translates into *ready to respond.*

When you get dressed in the morning, you trust a mirror

to tell you what you look like, and you are ready to respond depending on what you see. If the mirror tells you that your hair is messy and your shirt is wrinkled, you respond by brushing your hair and ironing your shirt. You don't analyze the validity of the mirror's image and say, "Well, let's define what is meant by the term 'wrinkled.' Maybe in this context it means whimsically arranged."

Nor do you procrastinate by processing your feelings about it and say, "I don't feel like my hair is messy. Brushing it just doesn't feel like it's coming from a sincere conviction. I want to be authentic in my grooming." That would be foolish.

You respond to what you see because you believe what the mirror is showing you. Your belief, or trust, in the reflection you see in the mirror results in a response. The book of James actually compares Scripture to a mirror that shows us what we really look like:

> Do not merely listen to the word, and so deceive yourselves. Do what it says. Anyone who listens to the word but does not do what it says is like someone who looks at his face in a mirror and, after looking at himself, goes away and immediately forgets what he looks like.[15]

When we look at the Scriptures, we find a reflection of what we look like in Christ. Let's be people who come ready to respond, and respond quickly.

When we respond in faith, this opens our minds to renewal and our life to transformation. The Bible says, "Do not conform to the pattern of this world, but be transformed by the renewing of your mind. Then you will be able to test and approve what God's will is—his good, pleasing and perfect will."[16]

When something is *con*formed, the same substance is molded into a new shape. But when something is *trans*formed, it becomes a different substance all together. Conformation is a response to some external force such as heat or pressure. It forces you to become what you are not. But transformation releases you to be to be the new creation you *truly are* in Christ.[17]

Transformation starts with changing how you think. We use the phrase "stuck in a rut" to describe stubborn habits and patterns that won't go away. We use the phrase "in a groove" to describe the positive momentum achieved by establishing desirable patterns and habits. Our thoughts, actions, and habits have the effect of creating grooves in our minds. The longer and more frequently we repeat a certain behavior, the more entrenched it becomes in our minds, lives, and personalities. This is true for both positive and negative behaviors.

Research shows that we can intentionally create new grooves in our brains in the same way the old ones were created. If you have gotten in a rut by dwelling on negative things and establishing destructive patterns, you can get your groove back by dwelling on positive things and establishing desirable patterns. "Be transformed by the renewing of your mind" is the way the Bible describes this process. By renewing your mind, you release the transforming power of God into your life. That's how we experience true and lasting change from the inside out.

The nature of God that has the power to transform us was deposited in us when we became members of God's family, but it is released as we renew our minds by learning to think the way God thinks.

"All Scripture is inspired by God and is useful to teach us what is true and to make us realize what is wrong in our lives," Paul told Timothy. "It corrects us when we are wrong and teaches us to do what is right. God uses it to prepare and equip his people to do every good work."[18]

We choose to believe in and respond to the reflection we see in God's Word, and in doing so, we establish his patterns of righteousness in our lives. Then, the Bible says, we will "approve" the good, acceptable, and perfect will of the Lord. "Approve" means to put something to the test to see how reliable and superior it is. When you put God's will and ways to the test against your own, you will find that his ways are good and perfect.

DEVOTIONAL ATTITUDE AND METHOD

An increasing revelation of Jesus and transforming truth are contained in the Scriptures, but we cannot access them without a decision to seek God's righteousness by spending time in the Word of God. Personal devotion is the daily practice of making room in your life to seek God through prayer and reading the Scripture. It doesn't have to take a long time. For most people it's only ten to twenty minutes. But the rewards of giving that time to God first will far outweigh the benefits of any other way you could choose to spend your time.

There are two important aspects of your approach to a daily time in God's Word: attitude and method. Understanding and applying both of these will make a huge difference in your daily devotion results.

Having the proper *attitude* is all about understanding that the Bible is God's infallible Word and that there is nothing equal to its authority. We can bring our questions to the Bible. We can bring our concerns to the Bible. But we must be careful about bringing our own agendas to the Bible. When we focus less on ourselves and simply allow the Bible to speak for itself, we position ourselves to experience God's revelation and lasting change in our lives.

The way you approach the Scripture, your *method*, is important too. There's nothing more helpful than following a simple Bible reading plan in your daily devotion. This is your navigation tool as you seek God in his Word. I personally recommend reading—are you ready for this?—only one chapter a day.

Most people, if they have ever attempted a yearly Bible reading plan, understand the challenges of trying to get through the whole Bible in a year. That comes to three or four chapters per day. Where do you find the time to read that many chapters every day? Even if you read all of the text, how can you process or meditate on all that you have read? Nobody, including me, can maintain that pace.

If you read one chapter a day, you can leave time and room to actually meditate on God's Word and allow God to speak to you. It can be relational that way. And you'll read through the entire Bible every three and a quarter years. How long did the disciples learn from Jesus, the Word who became flesh?[19] The same time—about three years.

Remember: it's not a checklist; it's an experience. We're after a relationship, not more information. We want to expose our hearts, not simply pack our heads.

I encourage you to read as much of the Bible as you can. But as a pastor, I've come to see over the years that if you're going to engage in prayer, meditation, and study of God's Word, you need to keep it simple and sustainable. I encourage you to consider using this plan. Even if you get behind a day or two, it is easy to catch up.

To get the most out of your devotional time, I recommend the following:

Bible. There are many different translations available, so be sure to get one that is easy for you to understand. In addition to the text of the Bible, a study Bible contains many tools to help you understand Scripture.

Journal. This is your spiritual DVR. It will be the place where you capture and record all of the good stuff God is doing and wants to speak into your life.

Scratch pad. This is different from your journal. It is for writing down all those little distracting things that come to mind while you're trying to focus on God. When something comes up, write it down and get it out of your mind. Make a "to do" list of things for later.

Place. It's helpful to set a specific time and place where you meet God each day. If you know when and where you plan to "meet God," you are more likely to show up. He will certainly be there waiting for you!

Once you have everything you need, carve out a quiet time each day to read one chapter and meditate. Take time reading, and allow God to speak to you. Highlight, underline, or place a mark in the margin of your Bible next to the Scriptures that stand out. When you are done, reread the verses you marked, look for one that particularly spoke to you that day, and write it in your journal. On the road to Emmaus, the disciples felt their hearts burning within them when Jesus spoke. What do you think God is saying to you in this Scripture? Ask the Holy Spirit to teach you and reveal Jesus to you. Paraphrase and write the Scripture down in your own words in your journal.

Now it's time to apply what you've learned. Personalize what you have read by asking yourself how it applies to your life right now. Perhaps it is instruction, encouragement, revelation of a new promise, or corrections for a particular area of your life. Capture in your journal how this Scripture can apply to you today. And consider memorizing some of the verses that speak to you the loudest. Write them in the back of your journal. Review them regularly, until you internalize them—until they become part of you.

Prayer comes next. This can be as simple as asking God to help you use this Scripture, or it may be a greater insight on what he may be revealing to you. Remember, prayer is relational. It's about connection. Don't just tell God what you see. Be sure to listen to what God has to say. Write down what he puts on your heart. And while you're at it, write down specific, answerable prayer requests. Date them and read through them regularly, reminding God of what you are trusting him for. When God answers each prayer, record the date—and celebrate!

As you begin to make time in God's Word a consistent part of every day, you will see and experience incredible growth and transformation in your personal life and walk with God. One of the powerful things that comes from journaling is seeing all the prayers God answers and miracles he performs in our lives.

Another great way to get more out of your time in the Word is to share your observations and applications with others. If you are having a time of regular daily devotion, you can then gather a group of family or friends and discuss the personal devotions you are reading or simply talk about what God is showing you during your devotional time with those you hang with through the week. Engaging in experiences like leading your very own devo group is a great next step in your commitment to a God-first life. Just like on the road to Emmaus, where two were walking together when Jesus appeared, sharing the journey by participating with one or more people will add a powerful element to the experience.

ARE YOU READY FOR GREATNESS?

Serve Others with Your Time and Resources

> Whoever wants to become great among you must be your servant ... just as the Son of Man did not come to be served, but to serve, and to give his life as a ransom for many.
>
> *Matthew 20:26, 28*

So many people are looking for greatness. No one wants an ordinary life anymore. This makes sense if you're a Christian because God is great and we're in God's family. But did you notice what Jesus did in the verse above? He's not pushing down that desire for greatness. But just as he did with happiness, he's redefining it for us. Jesus is showing us how to reach true greatness in his kingdom—by serving. Wanting to be great isn't bad. We're destined for greatness because we serve a great God. God just wants us to know what true greatness is.

I knew soon after I was saved that I was called to preach. Never mind that I hadn't preached a word yet. When I got the desire to serve God, I knew that's what God wanted me to do. Unfortunately, my pastor didn't get the same memo.

"I want to serve and help in any way I can," I said to him. "God's really been dealing with me about being a servant, and I want to obey."

I was sure Pastor would ask me to serve the Lord by preaching a message on servanthood to the college group during our weekly gathering on campus. Instead, he looked me up and down for a few seconds, sizing me up. Then he said, "Stovall, I'm so glad you came and offered to serve. I have been praying for someone to fill an important role in our Tuesday outreaches, and I think you would be perfect. In fact, I can't believe I didn't think of you before! This is an answer to prayer."

An "answer to prayer"! A role I was "perfect for"! Something he should have "seen all along"!

I knew it.

I was going to be the new speaker at our outreaches! Of course he could see the call of God on my life to preach and what a natural leader I was.

"Sure, Pastor," I said, "Whatever you need, I'm there."

"Great!" he said. "Show up at here at the church at ten in the morning every Tuesday. Reschedule your classes, because this is going to take all day, until at least two or three in the afternoon. And I need you to commit to this for the whole fall semester. Can you do that?"

"No problem!" I responded with enthusiasm, excited to finally get the opportunity I had been waiting for. "I'll do whatever it takes!" I couldn't believe this was happening. This was so much easier than I'd thought it would be.

"Okay then," he paused, a little taken aback by my enthusiasm. "So, when you get here, I need you to go to the storage room. Do you know that stage we do our outreach on every Tuesday?"

"You mean the one that's made up of those four huge wooden platforms? Um, yeah. Yeah, sure I do."

"I need you to get those and take them out to the student union for the outreach. And then, when it's over, I need you to pick them up, bring them back here, and put them in storage. I know they look big, but you're a strong guy. Lifting those things will be no problem at all for you. I can't imagine *why* I didn't think of you before now! Thanks, Stovall."

I must have stood there with my jaw dragging the ground a little too long, because he looked up at me and asked, "Do you have any questions?"

"Well, just one." This was *not* turning out at all like I thought it would. "Who's going to be the speaker at the outreaches?"

"Same guys as last semester. Is that all?"

"Yep. Yes, sir. That's about it."

I left my pastor's office that day about two feet tall. I thought about going back and trying to get out of it. Imagine — hauling wooden platforms back and forth. And now he expects me to change my class schedule? The nerve. If I had known that's what he was talking about, I would have said no.

But that's the problem right there.

I would have said no.

I'm glad I didn't. I'm glad I didn't walk back into my pastor's office and make up some lame excuse to get out of my commitment. Had I let pride keep me from fulfilling my commitment, there are things I never would have learned about myself. More importantly, there are things I never would have learned about Jesus. Even though he was the Son of God, the Bible says Jesus "made himself nothing" and took "the very nature of a servant" as his primary identity.[1]

If you're mind wasn't blown by away that thought, please go back and read it again. God is beyond awesome, beyond powerful. But God in Christ emptied and lowered himself. He set aside his power and position and stooped to serve us.

As we continue to put God first and seek his righteousness,

there are things about his nature and our journey with him we will never fully understand until we decide to lower ourselves and take on the identity of a servant.

THE SERVANT IDENTITY

Serving others as Christ served us goes beyond doing good deeds or giving our time and money for the kingdom—although that's important, and we'll spend some time later in the chapter talking about these things. Serving others starts with a shift in how we see ourselves. The God-first life means, among other things, laying down the privileges we have come to expect and being willing to see ourselves as servants first.

> Serving is not something we do; serving is who we are.

Serving is not something we do; serving is who we are. This is modeled by Jesus himself:

> Whoever wants to become great among you must be your servant, and whoever wants to be first must be your slave—just as the Son of Man did not come to be served, but to serve, and to give his life as a ransom for many.[2]

Notice how Jesus identifies his purpose. Jesus didn't see himself as a teacher, preacher, healer, or leader. He was all of those things and more, but Jesus, the Son of God, identified himself first of all as a servant.

Whatever you consider your primary identity—homemaker, businessperson, student—it's not your primary identity. You are a servant first, who has been given the opportunity to lead a business, care for your home, or influence your classmates. Whether it's preaching or hauling boards for a stage, we are called to serve. We are called to serve in many different ways, but all of them require giving something of ourselves. All of them require that we take on the character of Jesus—that we set aside our own goals, aims, and desires and give our time, talent, money, sweat, heart, and strength for the kingdom.

Something radical happens when we do this. By working with the local church, giving our tithes and offerings, offering our time and resources to missions and outreach, we build up

A SERVANT'S SELF-TEST

1. When someone assumes you will do the hard work, do you joyfully accept responsibility, or do you do it grudgingly and resentfully? *Servants expect to do the hard work.*

2. When you take up the extra slack, do you point it out to get the credit you deserve? Or are you satisfied by simply lifting the burden from another person's shoulders? *Servants say, "I have only done my duty."*

3. Imagine working under someone who you feel is less qualified than you. Do you challenge their authority to highlight their deficiencies and prove your own qualifications? Or do you work to bring success to the whole team? A football coach uses different personnel to manage different positions; the purpose is to get the right people in position to score. The team is more important than any individual's role. *Servants understand that the goal is more important than the role.*

4. Do you trade services or skills only for greater power in any given situation, holding out unless you get your way? Or do you give freely and without expecting anything in return? *Servants trade power for the privilege of seeing others succeed.*

the body and expand its reach. By putting the kingdom first, we make the kingdom grow. And something radical can happen in our hearts too. If we keep in mind that we serve others for the sake of Christ, then every effort we make, every sweat we break, every check we cut, every life we touch can be an act of worship.

I walked into my pastor's office that day thinking of myself as a leader who serves. But by the end of the semester, my perspective had been totally flipped. By the day of our last outreach, I saw myself as a servant who might have an opportunity to lead. If God wanted me to lead the outreach, he would have made that happen. But God was doing something bigger on the inside of me. Saying yes to God in service, even if it wasn't my favorite thing to do, was what God used to form Christ in me. The decision to *always* serve in my local church was one of the best decisions I ever made. And it's a key decision for us as we put God first.

WHERE WE FIT IN GOD'S ORGANIZATIONAL CHART

Have a look at the Servant's Self-Test. It's a good way to check your heart as it relates to service. If you are anything like me, you will see room for improvement. Don't let that discourage you. Jesus' disciples had such a difficult time embracing the role of a servant that he had to deliver one of the most famous illustrated sermons of all time just to show them how serious he was about it.

The Last Supper wasn't the first time Jesus spoke about serving, but it seems his students could never pass the test. They all wanted a place of power in his kingdom. They still had not figured out that Jesus' kingdom would not be established by throwing Rome from its place at the top of the ladder. He would instead lay down his life and *become* the ladder by which all people could reach the kingdom—even their enemies! So to make sure that they understood the organizational chart of his kingdom, he demonstrated it for them during his last few hours on earth.

John 13 tells us that Jesus left the table where the disciples were sitting. He took off his robe, grabbed a towel and wrapped it around his waist, filled a basin with water, and then proceeded to wash the feet of his disciples. In Jesus' day the outer robe signified a person's position in society. Jesus wore the robe of a rabbi, signifying his role as a teacher. It was an honored position in Israel. When Jesus took off his robe, he was laying aside the symbol of his earthly rank. He was sending a message: *Status does not define my disciples; servanthood does.*

Next, Jesus put on the servant's towel and washed his disciples' feet. In doing so, he redefined greatness just like he redefined happiness. In his kingdom, we climb down the corporate ladder to success by taking on the identity of a servant above whatever other role and position we may have in life.

One of the most unexpected things about this account of the Last Supper is the statement that leads into the foot-washing moment. "Jesus knew that the Father had put all things under his power, and that he had come from God and was returning to God."[3] *Jesus knew.* He knew the extent of his authority: *over everything.* He knew where he came from and where he was going: *from God and back to God.*

Jesus was secure. He was not having an identity crisis at this moment. He was not pandering to his disciples for affirmation. He was doing what he had always done, teaching them how to love one another. Serving like Christ means serving from a place of strength, not of insecurity, compulsion, or the need for approval. We never have to prove ourselves when our identity is rooted in Christ. Our worth is not in question; only the condition of our heart.

> Serving like Christ means serving from a place of strength, not of insecurity, compulsion, or the need for approval.

Are we willing to empty ourselves of everything we feel entitled to and serve like Jesus?

REACHING OUT

A few months ago, my wife, Kerri, noticed an elderly woman walking along a street near our neighborhood. She seemed disoriented and a little afraid. Kerri couldn't tell for sure, but she suspected this woman might be homeless.

Kerri was on the opposite side of the street, headed in the other direction in bumper-to-bumper traffic. She couldn't turn around quickly enough to get to the woman, but she prayed as she drove on: *Lord, please protect this woman and give her peace. And if there is any way that you can use me to serve her, please let me meet her again.*

A few weeks later, Kerri was hurrying to a meeting, and she pulled into a gas station to fill up her car. She answered texts while the tank was filling. Just as she took the nozzle out of the tank, she heard some footsteps shuffling in her direction. When she looked up, she saw the old lady she had prayed for a few weeks earlier. "Can you spare some money?" the woman asked. Recognizing this as an answer to her prayers, Kerri gladly said yes.

As she was going for her purse to take out some cash, Kerri felt the Holy Spirit prompt, *Ask her if she needs a ride.* Now Kerri was worried she would be late for her meeting, but still, she asked the woman if she needed a ride. The woman was relieved at the offer and asked for a ride to a nearby fast-food restaurant.

As she got in the car, Kerri noticed a gentleman who had been there all along filling his car at the next pump. He was smiling at the interaction he had just seen, nodding his head in approval. By now Kerri was feeling pretty good about herself. She had the lady in the car with her and was headed toward the restaurant, silently thinking about her meeting when the Holy Spirit prompted her again. *Ask her name. Talk to her. Notice her. Give her the dignity you would give anyone else.*

At this point Kerri recognized that God was testing the limits of her compassion. She had felt good about herself moments before, but now she realized she had a long way to go before she could start patting herself on the back. Her intent had been to just give some money and maybe a little extra time to the lady, not to get involved in any kind of personal way. The funny thing was, as Kerri began to talk to this woman, she stopped seeing her as a project she had taken on for the morning. She had a name: Cindy. She lived downtown but enjoyed the warmer beach air from time to time. She needed new gloves, and her legs ached when she walked for too long up and down the streets. If she had just a little bit more money, she could buy food for the week and not just lunch.

Kerri gave Cindy some more money. She prayed with her, talked to her about her plans for the day, and after a few minutes, went on to her meeting.

Later that night Kerri and I were talking about how that experience impacted her. "I forgot how much I love helping people," she told me. "I mean, I serve my family and I feel like my whole life is about helping people, because that's what the ministry is all about. But there was something about serving someone in a spontaneous, practical way that refreshed my soul. Following the prompting of the Holy Spirit in my daily routine to step out of my comfort zone and show the love of Jesus to a stranger he sent into my path was such joy."

Kerri also said that the situation showed her the limits of her compassion. "I was happy to give her money, but getting involved, giving myself, somehow made me uncomfortable," she said. "I realized that I hold back from helping people because I feel like I have to solve every single problem they have once I get involved. But today the most important thing I gave to Cindy was the dignity of simply asking her name. She didn't expect me to solve every problem. The help I gave her in that moment was appreciated, but the time we spent talking seemed to mean the most to her."

What happened to Kerri that day is a small picture of what happens to us when we go on a mission trip or participate in local outreaches. An important part of the God-first life is serving those who are in need, whether across the globe or in our own backyards. Many people are not only hurting from poverty and trials of life, but they also lack the hope they could have in Jesus. We are called to reflect the love of God and to serve our cities and our world by showing people they are not forgotten.

We love people wherever they are, no matter what season of life they're in and regardless of their physical, emotional, or economic status. Isn't that what God did for us? God loved us in our pride and shame and need. He wasn't trying to get something from us. God didn't come to us with an agenda or a quid pro quo. He just wanted what was best for us. He just loved us. And the Bible says that "we love because he first loved us."[4]

Reaching out is really the love of God in action, and it's a way for us to love like God does. God is a sender. He sent his Son, Jesus, into the world to redeem sinners like us. In turn, Jesus sends redeemed sinners like us out to reach the world. If the God-first life is about fulfilling the plans and purposes of God, then it means accepting the commission to reach the lost, feed the hungry, clothe the naked, visit the infirm, and reach the world.

THREE WAYS TO REACH OUT

The local church can reach communities in three ways: (1) meeting physical needs, (2) sharing the gospel, and (3) building up the local church.

1. *Meeting physical needs.* When Jesus was here on earth, he met people's physical and tangible needs. He fed the five thousand, healed the lame, restored sight to the blind, and took time to sit with a Samaritan woman to heal her soul. Perceiving and

meeting the needs of people was Jesus' way. Even when he was exhausted, Jesus' compassion for the hurting energized him to make a difference in every individual's circumstance.

More often than not, the meeting of a physical need prepared the way for an encounter with God. As people's bodies were made whole and their basic needs met, they began to open their hearts. As servants of Christ, we can follow Jesus' example and make a way for the Holy Spirit to get into the heart of the lost through the simple meeting of basic needs.

There might be several people in your world who have a physical need right now:

- a middle-school student in an at-risk area in the neighborhood who needs a mentor
- a single mom you know who needs help picking up groceries or fixing her car
- a homeless individual might need a jacket for a cold winter's night
- an elderly gentleman with much life wisdom might simply need a companion to listen

The beauty of meeting a physical need is that God uses this to soften hearts so people are open to hearing about Jesus. This brings us to one of the most powerful ways we can reach people.

2. *Sharing the gospel.* Jesus told his disciples, "You will receive power when the Holy Spirit comes on you; and you will be my witnesses in Jerusalem, and in all Judea and Samaria, and to the ends of the earth."[5] His directive is intentional here. They were to be witnesses locally (Jerusalem), regionally (Judea and Samaria), and globally (ends of the earth).

I spent much of my early twenties serving and planting churches on the mission field. One of the places I served the longest was the Amazon jungle. There was adventure there, yes, and it was exotic. But it's really important for us to understand that the church is called to be mission-focused not just to the remote jungles of Peru, but everywhere we can reach, at home and around the world.

3. *Building up the local church.* The local church is the vehicle that Jesus left on earth to be his hands and feet. Paul, the great builder of the local church, left this instruction: "The things you have heard me say in the presence of many witnesses entrust to reliable people who will also be qualified to teach others."[6]

The "reliable people" are those who will be faithful to carry out the work of the kingdom. After a short-term mission team departs a region, we want to ensure that long-term ministry continues. Without faithful people to continue and build the local church, those who experience the love and power of Jesus Christ will be left without the support needed to grow in Christ. Some of the ways we accomplish this are through building up global campuses, helping to equip others for more effective ministry, and serving in any capacity needed. Locally, we partner with other churches and seek to lift up the body of Christ wherever we serve.

When we serve, whether locally or globally, we are following in the footsteps of the greatest missionary of all time — Jesus. His mission on earth was to make an eternal impact in the life of every person. As you step out and get involved in local outreaches and global missions, you will experience what it is like to make a direct impact for the kingdom in the lives of those around your community and your world.

PUTTING GOD FIRST IN YOUR FINANCES

Now for the difficult one.

When people serve, they do so in several ways — offering their time, energy, skill, and money. Few people have a problem with the first three. But when it comes to letting go of money, that's a different story. Tithes and offerings seem like a struggle for most people. I get it, but I also wonder if there's a practical fact we all seem to forget when it comes to the church: organizations require resources to advance their mission and objectives.

Think of it this way. Universities require huge resources to finance higher education. Rarely will you hear a detractor say, "That school just wants all your money." It takes tremendous financial capital to run a political campaign, yet I have never heard either Republicans or Democrats complain that their political party has "raised too much money." Medical foundations for diseases such as cancer or AIDS need money to pay their research staff, but you would be hard-pressed to find a doctor or patient say the foundation wants "too much" of their money.

These educational, political, and medical organizations represent *causes* that their supporters believe in. But even good and noble causes like these have temporal value, while the church represents the greatest cause of all and has eternal value — reaching our world with the message of salvation through Jesus Christ! We shouldn't be suspicious when the church is successful. We should take it as confirmation. After all, the church is the only thing Jesus is building on earth, and he says that not even "the gates of Hades [can] overcome it."[7]

We have the honor of partnering with God to rescue humanity, and we step into that partnership when we recognize that advancing the gospel and reaching the lost require resources. There is a cost associated with every aspect of ministry, from administration to resources to communication. Being passionate about the mission of the church means fully embracing the shared responsibility to fund that mission. Jesus wants your entire heart, and the God-first life includes putting God first in everything, even our finances.

God is the source of all we have, and we trust God's

faithfulness to meet all of our needs. I've seen it time and again. I can't tell you the number of people I hear from at Celebration who make the decision to put God first in their finances and experience a profound breakthrough of God's blessing.

Luis, a disabled veteran in our church, was homebound after several tours in Iraq. He was struggling. But he decided to reach out way past his comfort zone and start tithing despite his circumstances, trusting God. Out of the blue he received a letter from the Veteran's administration. They'd made "a clear and unmistakable error" in his account. Do you know what came with that letter? A check for all the money they'd previously underpaid him. "I know this was no coincidence," Luis said. "God was showing me that his hand is at work in my life."

Though their first daughter had just been born, Christen and her husband, Lance, were almost near the end of their marriage. Finances were a part of their struggle, but in the midst of the trial, they made the decision to put God first. As part of that, they started tithing. God rewarded their trust. Not only did he heal their marriage, but he financially blessed them as well, enabling them to pay down their debts. "All because of God has this become possible," said Christen, "and we believe that God will continue to bless us!"

People report these stories all the time. There are many commonalities, but one thing is common in them all: these people decided to put God first. Nothing will yield greater blessing in your life than putting him first in your finances, and this starts with tithing.

TEN TRUTHS ABOUT TITHING

When we serve God with our money, the first step is tithing. The word *tithe* means "tenth," and when it comes to your money, your tithe simply refers to 10 percent of your income. Returning the tithe to God is an act of worship, one that positions you under an open heaven, protects you (and your finances) from the enemy, and channels abundance into your life. Here are ten things I like people to keep in mind about tithing.

1. *Tithing reminds us that the earth, and everything in it, belongs to God.* Everything we have has been given to us by God, including our jobs, our relationships, and especially our incomes. "Remember the LORD your God," Moses says in Deuteronomy, "for it is he who gives you the ability to produce wealth."[8] This means you are not an owner but a steward of everything you have, because it really belongs to God.

2. *Tithing is not only 10 percent of our income; it's the* first *10 percent.* God asks us to honor him with the "firstfruits of all your crops"[9]—which for most of us means our income. First means first. It's not what's left over after you've paid your bills, bought your groceries, and so on. You give to God before you give to anyone else, including yourself (savings), your creditors (bills), or even your government (taxes). Tithing your firstfruits tells God he's your first priority. In the Old Testament, God required people to give the firstborn of their livestock or the firstfruits of their harvest before they knew whether that animal would have any more offspring or whether they would get another crop. God was teaching them that they had to trust him in faith with their finances and trust that he would bless them more than they could ever bless themselves.

3. *The tithe is the "sacred portion" of our income and has tremendous power.* We see the power and influence of money everywhere we turn. But of all the money you have, it is your tithe that has the most power because it is sacred. "A tithe of everything ... belongs to the LORD," the Bible says; "it is *holy* to the LORD."[10] "Holy to the LORD" means that it is set apart for God's use, that it belongs to him. God extends blessing and favor over our lives through our tithes. Without that favor, we open ourselves to the devouring intentions of the enemy.[11]

Have you ever felt like your money was being devoured by financial emergencies? If you aren't tithing, you are vulnerable to Satan's plans to keep you from ever having a kingdom impact with your finances. Don't be fooled. Satan wants your money just as much as God does.

4. *Tithing is not giving. It's returning.* Malachi says, "Will a mere mortal rob God? Yet you rob me." How? God answers, "In tithes and offerings.... Bring the whole tithe into the storehouse, that there may be food in my house."[12] Withholding the tithe is not simply a passive decision to abstain from giving. It's theft. When we have a death grip on our tithes and refuse to release them, we are really struggling over the issue of ownership. When it comes to tithing, you really only have two choices. You can either return it to God or you can steal it.

5. *Your tithe is given to your local church.* Your church is where you've planted yourself, the place of your spiritual family, where you are serving and growing. Your local church is your "storehouse," or where you are fed spiritually. That's where God directs us to take our tithe.[13] You can offer additional gifts to important Christian ministries, missions, and charities, but the tithe belongs in your home church. Offerings are also for things like building programs, expansion initiatives, and other Christian endeavors. The church uses the tithe to advance the cause of Christ and to help meet the needs of the local community. The church leadership will give an account for how it is used, but you are blessed regardless.

6. *Tithing is an issue of obedience.* God asks us to tithe, and it is our responsibility to respond. Parents have to tell their children to obey—a lot. Sometimes they're fine with it; other times they're not. When my younger daughter, Annabelle, was two years old, she informed Kerri and me that she was less than thrilled with the concept of obedience. I had just finished telling her something she needed to do, and when she refused, I

added, "Annabelle, obey." She looked right at me and said, "I do not like that word." As far as God's concerned, that attitude is okay. Jesus tells the story of two sons, whose father gives them an order. One agrees but doesn't do it. The other grumbles but does it. "Which son obeyed?" asks Jesus. The answer is the one who grumbled but did what his father asked anyway.[14] Tithing is simply an issue of obedience or disobedience.

7. *Tithing is the one of the first steps of taking responsibility for your life.* When my children were younger, they would often leave personal items lying around the room or the house. Annabelle would typically leave her towel on the floor after taking a shower. She seemed to think the towel would magically pick itself up and get folded on its own. It was a real "aha!" moment for Annabelle when she realized she was responsible for picking up the towel. She soon recognized that if she didn't pick up the towel, someone else would need to. In other words, her irresponsibility was affecting not only her but also others. It's the same way when it comes to tithing. Tithing is the first step toward accepting your responsibility to advance the cause of Jesus. You want to hear God say to you, "Well done, good and faithful servant! You have been faithful with a few things; I will put you in charge of many things."[15]

8. *Tithing is a heart issue, not a money issue.* Three issues are emotionally at play when we struggle with the decision to tithe: trust, fear, and greed. In other words, it's not about the money — it's about what God is doing in our hearts. Sometimes giving makes no sense, but God still wants you to give. He's not doing this to make your circumstances more challenging, but to prove himself trustworthy and release provision and blessing into your life through your obedience. It can be easy to worry about giving, especially during tough economic times, but giving is actually the antidote to fear and worry. When we give, we are placing our confidence in God as our ultimate provider.

And greed doesn't stand a chance when we choose to be generous; we replace it with God, our true source of contentment.

9. *Tithing brings tremendous blessing.* The Bible says God "rewards those who earnestly seek him."[16] If there is anybody who knows how to reward and give good gifts, it's God! He loves to give good gifts to his children. Remember, 90 percent of your income with God's blessing goes a whole lot further than 100 percent without God's blessing.

10. *God established tithing to be a win-win-win situation.* God "wins" because he receives your worship through giving. You "win" because giving draws you into a relationship with Jesus as your Lord, and he will bless you in return. The church "wins" because the gospel can now be advanced and because there is food in the "storehouse" to reach more people for Christ.

Tithing is right because God expects it of us. But beyond that, it has real effects by delivering resources to kingdom work. Through our servanthood—every type of servanthood—God permits us to be a part of the great work he is doing in people's lives all around the world.

Is there risk in letting go? Is there risk in forfeiting our time, talent, and treasure, emptying ourselves like Jesus did to serve others? No. Not if you believe the God-first promise of Matthew 6:33. When we seek God's righteousness, "all these things" that we need "will be given to you as well." We're not entitled to anything, so it's an unfortunate game to act as if we are. We give and serve because God gives and serves, and we find that he blesses us far beyond whatever we try to do for ourselves.

PART 4

NEW FREEDOM

Seek first his kingdom and his righteousness, and *all
these things will be given to you as well.*

Matthew 6:33

FREE LIFE

Gain Real Freedom from the Past, in the Present, for the Future

It is for freedom that Christ has set us free. Stand firm, then, and do not let yourselves be burdened again by a yoke of slavery.

Galatians 5:1

The book of Philemon is the apostle Paul's shortest letter. Normally, he wrote to larger churches like those in Rome or Corinth, or to leaders of churches like Timothy or Titus. In these letters he explained the gospel, offered correction, and discussed replacing old life patterns with new, spiritual ones. We've referred to several of those writings throughout this book, but not the letter of Paul to Philemon.

Philemon lived in Colossae, where Paul had established a church. Philemon also owned a slave named Onesimus. We don't know much about what happened, but Onesimus apparently ran away and somehow ran smack dab into Paul while he was in prison in Rome—and you know Paul. He preached the gospel to Onesimus, who surrendered his life to God. Suddenly, here's this runaway slave and he's ministering with Paul in Rome.

But there was a reckoning coming. Paul knew that Onesimus couldn't stay with him forever. They still had to deal with Philemon at some point. This went beyond slave and master because this was ultimately about the fellowship of believers—about love and unity in the church. Somehow this runaway had to be reconciled with his master, who legally had the right to kill him. Thus, Paul wrote Philemon a letter, asking not only that he welcome Onesimus back but also set him free.

Onesimus carried that letter back home, and you can imagine the stress and worry that must have gone with him. It took a lot of faith for him to return. Again, Philemon could have had him killed for running away. What if Philemon didn't set him free? What if Philemon had wanted him dead? But miraculously, Onesimus returned to freedom. Philemon responded as Paul hoped.

I will come back to Onesimus's story shortly, but for now I want to emphasize that in this story, his past was forgiven, God was guiding his present, and he had hope for the future. The same things can be true for us. By seeking God's kingdom and righteousness first, we can know and experience freedom in every part of our lives. It comes from recognizing first and foremost that Christ lives in us. As we talked about in chapter 5, we have been given a new spirit, and with that spirit, incredible *power*—the power to overcome our past, to walk in fearless peace in the present, and to look to the future with joy, trusting God has a plan and purpose for our life.

Sometimes you may wonder, *I committed my life to Christ, so why do I still struggle with [insert personal issue here]?* It could be an issue of anger. It might be alcohol or substance abuse. Or it could be forgiving a close friend. We think we are "saved," and our new life in Christ should be easy and free of past sins. But we feel in bondage. We feel chained by some desire or impulse down inside us.

That's not the life that Matthew 6:33 promises. Even though it may not feel as if you're living in freedom now, you can know true freedom if you put God first in your life. Jesus said that when he sets us free, we are "free indeed," but so few people really seem free.[1] He did not free us from hell just to watch us live in it while we're on earth! This chapter will show you how to find the freedom of the God-first life.

But get ready to lean in a bit. We're going to get a little theological for a few pages. It might even feel like you're in therapy! Still, it's crucial to see that you have been set free on the inside. Freedom in the God-first life is all about your new inner freedom working its way out into the rest of your life.

UNCHAINING YOUR PAST

The first principle of God-first freedom is *freedom from the past*.

For every believer, regardless of background, the first engagement of spiritual growth is in dealing with the past. Everyone has a past, and few of us are proud of ours. Like Onesimus, there's trouble back there. Maybe you've come through a bad relationship, or maybe you've caused some hurt in someone's life. Whatever it is, we all have things we're not proud of, things that don't characterize the new life we're living.[2] Don't worry; you're in good company. The road to spiritual maturity starts with confession of sin and surrender to growth, and we all start out in the same place.

As I shared earlier, my life before Christ was marked by selfish pursuits, a lack of purpose, and a lot of sin and mess. There are many things I wish I could go back and do differently. I could have let myself be stuck in guilt and shame about those things, allowing emotions tied to the past to dictate my present. I could also have chosen to keep living my old life, dabbling in sin and disobedience. Instead, I accepted God's complete forgiveness of my sin by grace through Jesus and, next, broke through my old patterns of thinking, behaving, and choosing so that I was no longer a slave to those things in my new life.

We are made up of spirit, soul, and body, as we discussed in chapter 5. Our old nature — or "old self," as Paul called it — reflects our "sinful selves" before we were crucified with Christ and the negative patterns of thinking and behavior that can affect these three areas.[3] All of our past, present, and future sins are forgiven when we are born again. Our spirit is made whole in an instant, but our soul undergoes a transformation process called sanctification. This is where our ongoing struggles are being worked out.

Paul talked about this in his letter to the Romans. The spiritual side of him was seeking God's righteousness, but his natural side — his unsanctified side — kept tripping him up. "In my sinful nature," he said, "[I am] a slave to the law of sin."[4] But here's the good news:

> Therefore, there is now no condemnation for those who are in Christ Jesus, because through Christ Jesus the law of the Spirit who gives life has set you free.[5]

We come into this world with a sin nature — that is, a propensity for sin and disobedience. But the degree and scope of our sin and the effort it takes to overcome that old nature will greatly depend on how deeply imbedded our patterns of sinful thinking and behavior truly are. Putting God first means letting the Holy Spirit sift through the triggers for sin that have been shaped by our experiences.

From the time we are born, our soul (mind, will, and emotions) is programmed and shaped by our experiences. Everything we see, observe, learn, hear, and experience through our five senses is mapped out in the soul. Some of that learning is good, necessary, and intentional (like formal schooling). But a great deal of that programming is just plain toxic.

Everything from traumatic experiences (accidents, death, war, abuse), to generational patterns (behaviors adopted intentionally or unintentionally from family), to cultural patterns (prevailing ideas in our society)—all of these shape our conscience and program our mind and emotions in destructive ways. Sexual abuse in childhood, for example, warps the normal development of the soul. It fundamentally changes the way that a developing child will think, feel, and behave. A soldier returning from the horrors of war will have seen and experienced things that reshape the soul, and that soldier will look at the world through a new (and possibly distorted) mental and emotional lens.

When experiences like these are imprinted on an individual, the inevitable result is unhealthiness and injury to the mind, emotions, and will. See the problem? This vital part of the soul, which is responsible for making choices, is led to make those choices based on corrupted information. In most cases, this hurt soul goes on making those same unhealthy choices, establishing a pattern of sin and shame that continually repeats like a broken record. That pattern might lead to a coping pattern, such as drug or alcohol abuse, further fracturing the soul.

These tendencies toward wrong thinking, wrong behaving, and wrong choosing can run deep. We must be filled with the Holy Spirit so that those old patterns are erased and new, healthy, Spirit-led patterns are created. The Bible tells us to "throw off everything that hinders and the sin that so easily entangles. And let us run with perseverance the race marked out for us."[6] The power word in that reference is "entangles." Some translations read, "ensnares." To ensnare means to set a trap. When we fall into the trap of sin, we are bound to its consequences and pain. Thank God that Jesus can truly set us free and make us whole again.

We have to access the power of God within us to break old patterns, eradicate sin, reshape our thinking, and walk in freedom. Your soul is in a process of progressive sanctification.[7]

God won't be done with that great work until we see him in heaven, but be "confident of this, that he who began a good work in you will carry it on to completion until the day of Christ Jesus."[8]

There are some practical things you can do here. Start with your local church by finding the freedom or recovery ministry they offer. You'll be able to get some healthy counseling to identify your triggers, along with prayer for deliverance and freedom. You can also talk with one of your pastors about the next steps. At Celebration, our freedom ministry is one of the core ministries for helping our people find their way to health and restoration.

FREEDOM IN THE NOW

I had some older friends in ministry that had taken "executive physicals." When I was approaching my fortieth birthday, I thought maybe I should get one too. These physicals are thorough, they pretty much take the whole day, and one of the things included in these physicals is a full body diagnostic scan. These scans can detect a wide range of issues your body may be secretly harboring, and it seemed like a great idea to kick off my forties with the peace of mind of a clean bill of health.

I had every expectation that my scan would be normal. I'm in good physical shape, eat well, and work out regularly. Imagine my surprise when I was immediately hurried into the doctor's office as soon as my scan was finished and told by the physician that my scan had identified a critical health concern — I had a dangerously enlarged aortic root.

The aorta is the large, central artery that carries oxygenated blood from the heart and delivers it to the other major vessels of the body. As most people know, an enlarged artery (or aneurysm) *anywhere* in the body is a major concern, but an enlarged aorta is a bomb waiting to go off. Rupture of an aortic aneurysm in that location would mean sudden, irrevocable death. No 9–1–1. No resuscitation. Goodbye, earth. Hello, heaven. The physician told me my condition could be compared to running across a busy freeway blindfolded my entire life up to this point, and it was amazing that I had not been "hit." The fact that I had reached the age of forty without my aorta rupturing and killing me was, in his words, nothing short of a miracle.

I was told I needed immediate surgery, and I made rapid preparations with my church and family to step away from the pulpit and fly to Minnesota to have open-heart surgery. In the space of time between hearing my diagnosis and closing my eyes under anesthesia for my surgery (a period of a couple of days), there was plenty of time to contemplate my circumstances, and more than enough time to be consumed by worry, fear, and anxiety. But in those moments, even though there was legitimate concern for my health, I chose to operate from a position of trust in God and to accept the peace, even in the midst of a storm, that God offers when we trust him.

The second principle of God-first freedom is *freedom in the present.*

Through the grace of God in Jesus Christ we are forgiven and are free from the penalty of sin (past, present, and future) and free in our new spirit to walk in holiness, free from the patterns and behaviors of our old life. Even though we have a new life in Christ, we are still faced with temptation and are in a constant struggle against our flesh until the day we die or Jesus returns.

For the mature believer, many times these struggles begin with some type of fear. Whether it's the everyday pressure and pain that life dishes out, an unexpected health diagnosis like mine, the loss of a job, or the fact that the child who was just learning to walk yesterday is now driving your car for the first time (children kick our fears up to a whole new level, don't they?), fear is a natural part of life. But just because it's natural doesn't mean God wants us to be enslaved by it.

Healthy fear is meant to *protect* you, not *enslave* you. Fear is a God-given physiologic response to help us avoid and escape danger or harm. On a fundamental level, it is a survival response. It is natural and good for you to feel fear when you step onto a track and a train is hurtling toward you. Fear will drive your reaction and save your life. But fear generated by the adrenaline of dangerous circumstances is quite different from the fear we generate in our minds by indulging our doubts and disbelief that God will come through for us.

God tells us countless times in the Bible not to fear. Many Christians misinterpret "do not be afraid" to mean that they should not *feel* fear or that they should have no reason to fear, and yet Jesus himself said, "In this world you will have trouble. But take heart! I have overcome the world."[9] This means that we will face troublesome circumstances, and fear will be our natural response to those circumstances. It is impossible to control the emotion of fear when it comes upon you. God does not expect us to suddenly stop *feeling* fear.

In this life there will be many reasons to feel fear. It comes from living in a fallen and unpredictable world. But we serve a God who has overcome the world, and one of the major blessings of living a God-first life is freedom from fear in your present. The bigger context of Matthew 6 is all about being free from fear and worry. Matthew 6:33 is Jesus' direct response to fear and worry, and it is in him that we need to place our trust.

There are four symptoms of fear at work in your life:

1. Stress
2. Anxiety
3. Anger
4. Control

All of these emotional states are birthed from fear, and they fight against our freedom. These may not appear like fear on the surface, but deep down they are. They represent a deep concern that typically comes from fear of failure or fear of the unknown. Not knowing if you'll finish that big project by the deadline triggers the fear of potential failure, and the physiologic response to that fear is *stress*. *Worrying* about a teenage child who is out late on a Friday night is generated by the fear of the unknown: *Where is he? Why isn't she home yet? Has something happened?* And while *anger* may not seem to have a connection to fear, most anger stems from a fear of rejection — the rejection implied by not being listened to, agreed with, respected, obeyed, or valued. And whenever we're afraid, we often try to *control* people and problems to deal with our fear. It rarely works.

It's important to know that fear is a tool of the enemy. Satan would like nothing more than to keep you mired in stress, worry, and anger because if you're stuck in those ruts, you're not experiencing the freedom of the God-first life. As long as you remain paralyzed by fear, struggling with anger, wringing your hands in anxiety, or desperately trying to control everything and everyone in your hemisphere, Satan will have you right where he wants you. But putting God first means positioning ourselves where God wants us — and God wants us walking in fearless peace.

Fear is the opposite of faith and love. "There is no fear in love," the Bible says. "But perfect love drives out fear."[10] God is perfect love, which means the presence of God dispels, or drives away, all fear. The presence of God in us, the presence of his perfect love, is the power we need to dispel fear. But we fear in places where we either don't know or don't trust the love of God.

When God's Spirit came to reside in you and you were given all you needed for "life and godliness," you were given in that moment all that you needed to set aside fear and to walk freely in faith. "God has not given us a spirit of fear," Paul says, "but of power and of love and of a sound mind."[11] The problem is that for most of us, fear has ruled our souls for many years and for many reasons, and letting go of that fear to trust the God we've just accepted can be difficult and painful. But we'll never know freedom until we do.

Fear manifests itself in stress, worry, anxiety, anger, and control, but it originates from some deep and complex roots and, if not pruned, will only grow. No amount of therapy, self-help techniques, or meditation will eradicate it. Again, only *perfect love* can cast out fear. Without God, any effort to do this on your own will be fraught with frustration. "Apart from me," says Jesus, "you can do nothing."[12]

Uprooting fear, worry, and anxiety will come from your willingness to identify your fears and surrender them to God. "Cast all your anxiety on him because he cares for you," says Peter.[13] If you give those fears to God, the more opportunities God will have to show you that he is faithful, and the more he proves himself faithful, the more your trust in him will be built.

Let's take this back to the story of Onesimus. Paul's letter to Philemon is short, and it only gives us part of the story. Several years later the leader of the church in Antioch, a man named Ignatius, wrote a letter to the church at Ephesus, a city near Colossae. Who should pop up in that letter but Onesimus! Now we find out that he's a leader in the church there. Catch that? Whatever fears or worries Onesimus felt as he was heading home to Philemon, God had set him free already—free from his old life first and then free in a new life and ministry.

FUTURE HOPE

The third principle of God-first freedom is *freedom for the future.* Let's face it, one of the primary areas where Christians struggle with trusting God is the future.

We can have confidence in our ultimate outcome—an eternity in heaven with God—but beyond that, the future is an unknown. We don't know the mind of God, so we are not always able to see his plans or the obstacles and opportunities that lie ahead of us. In the previous section, I discussed the strong tie between worry and fear of the unknown. We can expend a lot of mental and emotional energy worrying about what will happen tomorrow, or next week, or ten years from now. But what good does it really do to be anxious in the present?

Instead of our worrying, Jesus gave us a simple example to learn from. Birds and flowers don't work, or toil, or worry; yet God provides for them and adorns them with beauty. Jesus goes on to say,

> Are you not much more valuable than they?... So do not worry, saying, "What shall we eat?" or "What shall we drink?" or "What shall we wear?" For the pagans run after all these things, and your heavenly Father knows that you need them. But seek first his kingdom and his righteousness, and all these things will be given to you as well. Therefore do not worry about tomorrow, for tomorrow will worry about itself. Each day has enough trouble of its own.[14]

Jesus gives the God-first text of Matthew 6:33 in the context of how people are bound by fear and worry over the things of this life. Matthew 6:33 is the antidote. It is our passport to true freedom in this life. It provides an authentic freedom over all the things that enslave the hearts and minds of humanity.

It isn't the circumstances of life that weigh us down—it's the worry over those things that zaps us of our strength. Without God, nonbelievers will run around trying to meet all their needs, cover all their bases, and manage every outcome. And they will be stressed out, sleep deprived, and depleted.

When you worry, you get weary. Being anxious about your finances will rob you of your sleep. Being consumed by anger and bitterness will steal your attention and your focus. Anger also displaces your joy, which in turn deprives you of strength.[15] All of these things bind you. They take something from you. They deplete your strength, your focus, your enthusiasm, and your motivation.

How do you put God first when it comes to your own fear, worry, and stress? You have to trust God enough to put those things in his hands. "Come to me, all you who are weary and burdened, and I will give you rest," said Jesus.[16] Rest doesn't come from operating under a spirit of fear. Rest doesn't come from dwelling in worry. Rest doesn't come from trying to control everything. How can you truly rest if simmering beneath the surface at all times is a well of stress, worry, or anger?

Rest comes from trusting God for our future. The first step is to turn our circumstances over to God, to exchange our burdens for his peace. "Take my yoke upon you and learn from me," says Jesus, "for I am gentle and humble in heart, and you will find rest for your souls. For my yoke is easy and my burden is light."[17] Jesus is telling us clearly that his yoke, the burden of following him and trusting him, is light. In exchange for surrender and trust, we will be given rest for our souls—that is, rest for the mind, rest for the emotions, and rest from the strife of advancing your own will over God's will. You can't start trusting God until you start putting those worries in his hands.

As the father of three children, I give a great deal of thought to the future and how it will impact my family, both in the immediate and the long term. What will the world be like for my children when they are grown? What about my grandchildren? In an increasingly fallen world, it is human nature (even more so for a person of faith) to have anxiety over the future.

Perhaps you are worried about how you will pay for your kids' college. Or you could be struggling with the ever-present anxiety of a retirement that is rapidly approaching and wondering how you'll face it without the prospect of a comfortable "nest egg" and a great investment portfolio. Just like the worry and fear for the present, worry over the future is a matter of trust. The same God who is providing for your needs in the "here and now" will provide for them in the "there and then."

The Bible assures us that God "will meet all your needs according to the riches of his glory in Christ Jesus."[18] Notice it said *all*? Guess what. That means God has "the riches of his glory" laid up to meet even the needs you don't have yet! Experiencing true peace about the future comes from trusting that it's all in God's hands. "I know the plans I have for you," God says, and these are "plans to prosper you and not to harm you, plans to give you hope and a future."[19]

The God-first life is not a life trapped in sin and pain, a life burdened by stress and anxiety about money or obligations, or a life defined by worry and uncertainty about the future. Remember, God's righteousness — his way of doing things — requires *trust*. God has not called you to try and figure everything out, nor has he equipped you to have a fulfilling life apart from him. He knows we need freedom from our past, freedom in the present, and freedom for the future, and Matthew 6:33 promises that we can have it by living a God-first life.

FIRST THINGS FIRST

The Choice Before You: Will You Put God First Today?

Be strong and courageous. Do not be afraid; do
not be discouraged, for the LORD your God will be
with you wherever you go.

Joshua 1:9

We were going down the Amazon in a longboat. Water curled
off the sides of our boat as we cut along the murky currents. It
was a long trip down river, twenty-five miles from Puerto Mal-
donado to a remote village in the Amazon. Before I became the
lead pastor of Celebration Church, I was college and young-
adult pastor at a church in Louisiana. It was my first big mission
trip to lead, and I was leading several kids from our college and
young-adult ministry. We all took in the scenery and tried to
spot animal life in the dense jungle on either side of the river.
I prayed that God would move in us and that the trip would
teach us new things.

The boat was crowded. Not only did I have twenty-
five young adults on board, but there were several locals as well:
a young woman with a nursing baby, the pilot of the boat, and a
young man perched on the prow looking out for obstructions
in the river.

He didn't spot it, but I did. A huge rock was right under the surface of the water, just about fifty yards ahead. We had plenty of time to steer clear of it. I didn't say anything, assuming that at any moment, the guy upfront would yell back to the pilot, who would then nudge us out of harm's way. But he remained quiet.

As the distance closed between us and the rock, I got nervous. Truthfully, I was a bit uneasy about saying anything. Here I was an inexperienced pastor from the U.S. What did I know about navigating the Amazon? These guys were not only locals; they were professionals. Surely they knew something about avoiding rocks in the river. The guy upfront would say something any second now.

Maybe now.

Or ... now?

But, no. Not a peep.

I couldn't stand it any longer and finally blurted something out. But it was too late. The pilot pushed the rudder, but we were already on the rock. And just as fast, the bow shot up and over to the right, pitching all of us into the river before the boat capsized.

Here we were on my first big mission trip, and all my kids were going to drown on my watch. Or be eaten—after all, there are piranha in the Amazon, along with anaconda and black caiman. If you've seen *Animal Planet*, you know what I'm talking about. All I could think was, *Lord, help us.*

When I got my head above water I could see the kids here and there, bobbing this way and that, carried by the current. There were screams and shouts. I could see the pilot was trying to turn the boat over.

And the baby! I suddenly remembered seeing the mother and baby thrown from the boat as well. I thrashed one way and then another, trying to see if I could find them. Praise

God—there was the mama. She was holding the baby above her head and fighting to keep her own head above the low waves. I swam to her as fast as I could. Just as I got to her, the boat pulled alongside us. I grabbed the infant with one hand and the boat with the other and tried to help the baby on board, but I couldn't.

Amid all the chaos and disorder, the baby was visibly calm. But it had a grip on his mama's hair like I couldn't believe. He just wouldn't let go. Somehow he knew that the only safe place in all that confusion was with his mother, and nothing was going to come between them if he could help it.

After some struggle I was finally able to get the child aboard the boat. The one thing I remember was his mama's black hair. The baby had giant a clump of it in his tiny fist. He held on to her with everything he had.

Some of the kids were now swimming to the boat, and once Mama and the rest nearby were onboard, we rushed to pick up the kids still in the water. At last, everybody was back on the boat. No one drowned. The piranha, anaconda, and caiman all went hungry that afternoon. Still, the whole episode shook me up for days. It could have been disastrous.

As I kept reflecting on what had happened, God taught me something—just as I had asked him in prayer. The lesson didn't come from not speaking up (though next time, I certainly will) or from the fright of watching the kids bob down river (do they make piranha repellant?). Actually, the lesson came in that little baby's fistful of his mama's hair. He was just a tiny thing, but he knew how to order his world. He knew how to lay hold of Mama. It was instinctual for him, and so the danger and the chaos had no effect on him. He just held on to Mama. Everything would work out if he just held on to Mama.

The message of the God-first life came back to me. In fact, it drove it home in a fresh and powerful way. Life is crazy, and half the time you're fighting to keep your head above water. The only answer is to trust God and keep holding on to him. Keep putting him first, no matter what. Everything else will work out when we keep our kingdom priorities.

DON'T FORFEIT YOUR BLESSING

Have you ever noticed that the first thing God spoke to Adam and Eve was a blessing? When he created Adam and Eve and placed them in the garden, God blessed them with the following words: "Be fruitful and increase in number; fill the earth and subdue it. Rule over the fish in the sea and the birds in the sky and over every living creature that moves on the ground."[1]

We all know this story, but we can miss the full impact of those words. There are a lot of things that God could have done to make a first impression on the human race. He could have awed Adam and Eve with great displays of power. Seriously, can you imagine how they would have reacted if God had shown up in a tricked-out chariot and wowed them with some celestial fireworks? He could have. He's God. Or he could have scared them with threats about what would happen if they displeased him. He could have started off by going over all the house rules. But he didn't. God's first words to Adam and Eve showcased his goodness.

Here's the other amazing thing about that verse: the blessing was woven together with purpose. God had a vision for the earth. He wanted the world to be full of people and bursting with life. He commissioned Adam and Eve to carry out his plans. Their work brought them purpose and a valuable place in the world. It gave them the opportunity to stretch their creative capacity to the limits and build a civilization *with God*! God gave humanity the opportunity to create with him. He wanted them to experience the fulfillment of a day's work, the satisfaction of seeing an inner vision become a reality.

God saw fit to let his creation become creators in their own right, and it was part of his joy to watch them multiply the seed he had given them. The desire to be happy and fulfilled was not Adam and Eve's idea. Happiness and fulfillment are God's ideas, and he knows best how to bring those things into your life.

The blessing that God gave Adam and Eve applied not only to them but also to everything God placed under their rule. He gave them the mission, the power, and the drive to create such a world—under his authority. Of course, this is where the true problem came in. God gave Adam and Eve authority over the created world, but he reserved the place of ultimate authority over all things—people included—for himself.

The commandment God gave about the tree of knowledge of good and evil was never actually about the fruit or even about eating the fruit. It was all about who was first, and as long as God was first, blessing and fruitfulness were just the normal course of life. When Adam and Eve ate the forbidden fruit, they were choosing to step into God's place. The problem was, once they made that choice, they found they did not have what it took to get the job done.

In God's created order, humanity flourished in their place under God's authority. The tragedy of Adam and Eve is that they tried to find their life outside of God. When they stepped into God's place—first place—things fell apart. An ordered world quickly unraveled, and disorder and its fruits (worry, stress, toil, pressure, pain) became the norm of the day for humanity. Things that were initially meant to bless them became a curse to them. Adam's "job" became a source of stress. Eve's role as mother and wife became painful and complicated. The blessed union of marriage became prone to power struggles. When order was disrupted, blessing was disrupted too.

Isn't that also our tragedy?

151

THE POWER OF DECISIONS

We experience the same consequences today when we try to step into God's shoes or put other things in the place that he alone can fill. When we step into first place, we discover that, just like Adam and Eve, we don't have what it takes to hold our world in place. We may experience success or acquire great wealth, but in the back of our minds, we are taunted by the persistent nagging threat that it might not last. Or we might find ourselves on the opposite end of the spectrum, consumed with worry over how to make ends meet, longing for peace but unable to grasp it. The things that start off as blessings—our jobs, relationships, homes, and even our money—become constrictive bonds when we put our trust in those things instead of God.

When you choose to live the God-first life, you are making the choice to restore order. Not things first, stuff first, or me first, but God first. When order is restored, blessing is released.

You will find that a world where you are not at the center is a world where happiness and blessing can be experienced— God's way. The truth is that "first" is not a place you can fill; it never was and it never will be. As long as you rule your world, the weight of it will fall on your shoulders, but when you step aside and let God step into his rightful place, the weight of your world falls on his shoulders. In the end, he is the only one who is truly able to hold it in place.

Everything around us and within us tells us that the secret to happiness is a world where it's all about me. But Jesus consistently says the opposite. True success is not a world where I am at the center but a world where God is at the center and my life is in proper order. First place belongs to God alone.

Why do so few people in the body of Christ experience true blessing and freedom? They may no longer be bound in sin, but they are trussed up by the cares of this life—the baggage of their past, the worries of the present, and anxiety about the future. They are repeating old patterns, behaviors, and habits that shaped them in their old life, not realizing (or having forgotten) that God has given them everything they need to walk away from those things.

The God-first life comes down to decisions. Adam and Eve decided not to put God first. Faced with a choice that looked tasty and attractive and would put them in the know, they bit. And we do too if we forget that we're not in the choosing game. We've decided, and now we need to simply maintain, what we've already committed to:

- I will make God's family my primary family.
- I will engage in the community life of the church.
- I will be filled by the Spirit.
- I will worship God on my own and with my church family.
- I will spend time with God through prayer and his Word.
- I will give of myself and my means.
- I will experience the freedom, joy, and blessing that God offers.

Paul tells us to "hold firmly to the word of life."[2] These decisions help us do that. They enable us to keep things in the order that God desires for us. We don't renegotiate them or trade them for other things on offer, no matter how attractive. When order is restored, blessing is released. If we blow the order, we've blown the whole thing. My mind keeps going back to that baby. He could have gone off in any number of directions. The current was strong, and there was chaos all around. But he was fixed. These decisions are like that powerful and determined grip.

How strong is your grip?

TAKE A SWING

When I was about ten years old, I played baseball on a Little League team. I was not a very good baseball player—at least I wasn't a good hitter. There was something about going up to bat that freaked me out. Every time the pitcher released the ball, I froze. I wanted to walk every time, so I just wouldn't swing the bat. In the last game of the season we were down by two runs in the last inning of the game. There were two outs, and the bases were loaded. And guess who was up to bat?

I heard the coach call my name, and instantly a wave of trauma-induced nausea swept over my body. I knew that I was a terrible hitter and that I would strike out and lose the game. I saw my future as fifth-grade loser, and it wasn't pretty. Sure enough, I got up to the plate, and when the pitcher threw the first pitch, I froze just like every other time.

Strike one.

I could see my teammates and coaches looking at me in despair, and I started crying. I didn't want anybody to see me, so I stepped away from the plate and put my head down. When I turned around and looked back, standing against the fence was my dad. Like lots of Little League dads, he usually got pretty passionate about the games. His face was pressed into the chain-link fence, and he looked like he wanted to climb through. So I walked up to my dad, and through my tears I said, "Dad, I don't think I can do this. I'm going to lose the game."

"Son, look at me," my dad said. I looked up into my dad's eyes as he continued, "Son, listen. I love you. You can do this, but you've got to take a swing." As I turned around and slowly walked back to the plate, I heard him call after me, "Don't worry about the pitch, whether it's high or low, inside or outside. Just take a swing!"

And I'll never forget what happened next. It seemed like it

all happened in slow motion. I walked right back into the batter's box. The pitcher threw the next pitch. I didn't know if it was a ball or a strike, high or low, left or right—I can't even remember. All I remember is thinking, *I'm going to swing as hard as I can, no matter what.* And that's what I did.

Crack!

I had never heard such a sound at the plate. It was almost deafening. I stood there in a daze of disbelief for a few seconds, until the voices of my teammates snapped me back to reality. "Run! Run! Run, Weems! Run!" my teammates shouted. I looked up and saw them sprinting around the bases and jumping up and down. I hadn't just hit the ball. I had just hit a game-winning, grand-slam home run.

I will say it again—we have been given "everything we need for a godly life."[3] Life is going to throw you some curve balls, and you may think you're the most inept person ever to step up to the plate of life. But God has put you at the plate with Matthew 6:33. All you have to do is take a swing.

Make the decision once and for all that you will live a God-first life. What have you got to lose? If you take this swing, God will take care of the rest. As you live with God first, one day you will look back on your life and realize it was a grand-slam home run by God's grace and power.

NEW TESTAMENT COMMANDMENTS

In chapter 3, I mentioned that there are several New Testament commands you are incapable of obeying unless you are planted in a local church. Here is a sampling of those commands.

MUTUAL MINISTRY

The one who receives instruction in the word should share all good things with their instructor. (Galatians 6:6)

Since you excel in everything—in faith, in speech, in knowledge, in complete earnestness and in the love we have kindled in you—see that you also excel in this grace of giving. (2 Corinthians 8:7)

Each of you should give what you have decided in your heart to give, not reluctantly or under compulsion, for God loves a cheerful giver. (2 Corinthians 9:7)

SPIRITUAL GIFTS

Do not neglect your gift, which was given you through prophecy when the body of elders laid their hands on you. Be diligent in these matters; give yourself wholly to them, so that everyone may see your progress. (1 Timothy 4:14–15)

In the presence of God and of Christ Jesus, who will judge the living and the dead, and in view of his appearing and his kingdom, I give you this charge: Preach the word; be prepared in season and out of season; correct, rebuke and encourage—with great patience and careful instruction. (2 Timothy 4:1–2)

You, however, must teach what is appropriate to sound doctrine. (Titus 2:1)

Each of you should use whatever gift you have received to serve others, as faithful stewards of God's grace in its various forms. (1 Peter 4:10)

But the one who prophesies speaks to people for their strengthening, encouraging and comfort. Anyone who speaks in a tongue edifies themselves, but the one who prophesies edifies the church. (1 Corinthians 14:3–4)

If anyone speaks in a tongue, two—or at the most three—should speak, one at a time, and someone must interpret. If there is no interpreter, the speaker should keep quiet in the church and speak to himself and to God. Two or three prophets should speak, and the others should weigh carefully what is said. (1 Corinthians 14:27–29)

So Christ himself gave the apostles, the prophets, the evangelists, the pastors and teachers, to equip his people for works of service, so that the body of Christ may be built up. (Ephesians 4:11–12)

EVANGELISM AND DISCIPLESHIP

Therefore, my dear brothers and sisters, stand firm. Let nothing move you. Always give yourselves fully to the work of the Lord, because you know that your labor in the Lord is not in vain. (1 Corinthians 15:58)

He is the one we proclaim, admonishing and teaching everyone with all wisdom, so that we may present everyone fully mature in Christ. (Colossians 1:28)

Then Jesus came to them and said, "All authority in heaven and on earth has been given to me. Therefore go and make disciples of all nations, baptizing them in the name of the Father and of the Son and of the Holy Spirit, and teaching them to obey everything I have commanded you. And surely I am with you always, to the very end of the age." (Matthew 28:18–20)

ENCOURAGEMENT AND FELLOWSHIP

Brothers and sisters, if someone is caught in a sin, you who live by the Spirit should restore that person gently. (Galatians 6:1)

Be shepherds of God's flock that is under your care, watching over them—not because you must, but because you are willing, as God wants you to be; not pursuing dishonest gain, but eager to serve; not lording it over those entrusted to you, but being examples to the flock. (1 Peter 5:2–3)

You who are younger, submit yourselves to your elders. All of you, clothe yourselves with humility toward one another, because "God opposes the proud but shows favor to the humble." (1 Peter 5:5)

Do not be yoked together with unbelievers. For what do righteousness and wickedness have in common? Or what fellowship can light have with darkness? (2 Corinthians 6:14)

... not giving up meeting together, as some are in the habit of doing, but encouraging one another—and all the more as you see the Day approaching. (Hebrews 10:25)

NOTES

CHAPTER 1: YOUR LIFE, GOD'S WAY

1. Psalm 37:23: "The LORD makes firm the steps of the one who delights in him."
2. Matthew 11:28: "Come to me, all you who are weary and burdened, and I will give you rest."
3. Psalm 19:7 – 8: "The law of the LORD is perfect, refreshing the soul. The statutes of the LORD are trustworthy, making wise the simple. The precepts of the LORD are right, giving joy to the heart. The commands of the LORD are radiant, giving light to the eyes."
4. Romans 8:28: "And we know that in all things God works for the good of those who love him, who have been called according to his purpose."
5. 1 Corinthians 2:9: "What no eye has seen, what no ear has heard, and what no human mind has conceived—the things God has prepared for those who love him."
6. 1 Peter 1:18 – 19: "For you know that it was not with perishable things such as silver or gold that you were redeemed from the empty way of life handed down to you from your ancestors, but with the precious blood of Christ, a lamb without blemish or defect."
7. Hebrews 13:5: "God has said, 'Never will I leave you; never will I forsake you.'"

8. Psalm 18:1–2: "I love you, LORD, my strength. The LORD is my rock, my fortress and my deliverer; my God is my rock, in whom I take refuge, my shield and the horn of my salvation, my stronghold."
9. Jeremiah 29:11: " 'For I know the plans I have for you,' declares the LORD, 'plans to prosper you and not to harm you, plans to give you hope and a future.' "
10. Philippians 4:7: "And the peace of God, which transcends all understanding, will guard your hearts and your minds in Christ Jesus."
11. Romans 15:13: "May the God of hope fill you with all joy and peace as you trust in him, so that you may overflow with hope by the power of the Holy Spirit."
12. James 5:13: "Is anyone among you in trouble? Let them pray. Is anyone happy? Let them sing songs of praise."
13. Steven Levy, "Good for the Soul," *Newsweek*, October 16, 2006, http://allaboutstevejobs.com/sayings/stevejobsinterviews/newsweek06.php (accessed September 4, 2013).
14. Romans 8:15–17: "The Spirit you received does not make you slaves, so that you live in fear again; rather, the Spirit you received brought about your adoption to sonship. And by him we cry, '*Abba,* Father.' The Spirit himself testifies with our spirit that we are God's children. Now if we are children, then we are heirs—heirs of God and co-heirs with Christ, if indeed we share in his sufferings in order that we may also share in his glory."

CHAPTER 2: ORDER AND BLESSING

1. Daniel Schorn, "Tom Brady: The Winner," CBSNews. com, February 11, 2009, http://www.cbsnews.com/stories/2005/11/03/60minutes/main1008148.shtml (accessed September 4, 2013). Original *60 Minutes* segment broadcast November 6, 2005, updated December 20, 2007.
2. Proverbs 10:22.

3. Colossians 1:18, italics added.

4. Psalm 37:4.

5. Matthew 18:4: "Therefore, whoever takes the lowly position of this child is the greatest in the kingdom of heaven."

6. Matthew 20:26–27: "Whoever wants to become great among you must be your servant, and whoever wants to be first must be your slave."

7. Matthew 6:19, 25: "Do not store up for yourselves treasures on earth, where moths and vermin destroy, and where thieves break in and steal ... Therefore I tell you, do not worry about your life, what you will eat or drink; or about your body, what you will wear. Is not life more than food, and the body more than clothes?"

8. Matthew 6:31–33.

9. Todd D. Hunter, *Our Favorite Sins* (Nashville: Thomas Nelson, 2012), 23, 239–40. See also: "New Research Explores the Changing Shape of Temptation," Barna Group, January 4, 2013: www.barna.org/barna-update/culture/600-new-years-resolutions-temptations-and-americas-favorite-sins (accessed September 4, 2013).

10. Mark 4:18–19.

CHAPTER 3: ADOPTED INTO GOD'S FAMILY

1. Jeremiah 17:7–8.

2. Hebrews 10:12–14, emphasis added.

3. Psalm 92:12–15.

4. Galatians 6:2.

5. Matthew 16:18.

6. Ephesians 5:25.

CHAPTER 4: DOING LIFE TOGETHER

1. Acts 2:41–47.

2. Matthew 18:20.

3. 1 Corinthians 12:12–31.

4. Proverbs 27:17, NLT.

5. Romans 12:15, NLT.

6. James 5:16a.

7. James 5:16b.

8. John Wesley, Sermon 24, Wesley Center Online, http://wesley.nnu.edu/john-wesley/the-sermons-of-john-wesley-1872-edition/sermon-24-upon-our-lords-sermon-on-the-mount-discourse-four/ (accessed September 5, 2013).

CHAPTER 5: DON'T HIDE YOUR TREASURE

1. Matthew Healey, "Once-Maligned Coin Nears Its Big Payday," *New York Times*, April 14, 2013, www.nytimes.com/2013/04/15/us/1913-liberty-head-nickel-is-expected-to-fetch-millions.html (accessed September 6, 2013).

2. "Rare nickel goes for $3.1M at auction," CBSNews.com, 26 April 2013, www.cbsnews.com/8301-201_162-57581551/rare-nickel-goes-for-$3.1m-at-auction/ (accessed September 6, 2013).

3. Colossians 1:27.

4. Ezekiel 11:19: "I will give them an undivided heart and put a new spirit in them"; 36:26: "I will give you a new heart and put a new spirit in you."

5. 1 Peter 1:23: "For you have been born again, not of perishable seed, but of imperishable, through the living and enduring word of God."

6. 2 Corinthians 5:17.

7. John 7:38.

8. Galatians 3:3.

9. 2 Corinthians 4:7, NKJV.

10. Romans 7:6.

11. See Matthew 15:19; 1 Corinthians 6:9–10; Galatians 5:19–21; Colossians 3:5; 1 Timothy 1:9–10.

12. 1 Corinthians 6:11.
13. Ephesians 4:22–24.
14. Galatians 5:22–23, NIV (1984).
15. Galatians 4:19, emphasis added.
16. Hebrews 10:14.
17. Ephesians 5:18.
18. Galatians 5:16, NLT.
19. Luke 11:11–13: "Which of you fathers, if your son asks for a fish, will give him a snake instead? Or if he asks for an egg, will give him a scorpion? If you then, though you are evil, know how to give good gifts to your children, how much more will your Father in heaven give the Holy Spirit to those who ask him!"
20. James 2:17.
21. Galatians 5:25, NLT.
22. Zechariah 4:6.
23. Proverbs 4:23.

CHAPTER 6: SPACE FOR THE SOUL TO BREATHE

1. Psalm 40:2–3.
2. 2 Peter 1:3.
3. David Kinnaman, *You Lost Me* (Grand Rapids: Baker, 2011), 116.
4. Luke 4:18–19.
5. John 4:10, 14.
6. John 4:23.
7. Malachi 1:11.
8. 2 Chronicles 5:11–13.
9. 2 Chronicles 5:13–14, NLT.
10. Zechariah 2:13.
11. 1 Corinthians 6:19: "Do you not know that your bodies are temples of the Holy Spirit, who is in you, whom you have received from God?"

12. 2 Chronicles 20:12, 15.

13. 2 Chronicles 20:21.

14. 2 Chronicles 20:24–25.

15. Ephesians 6:12: "For our struggle is not against flesh and blood, but against the rulers, against the authorities, against the powers of this dark world and against the spiritual forces of evil in the heavenly realms"; Colossians 2:15: "Having disarmed the power and authorities, he made a public spectacle of them, triumphing over them by the cross."

16. Psalm 22:3, NLT.

17. 2 Chronicles 20:26, NLT.

18. Luke 10:27.

19. Psalm 47:1, 6.

20. Colossians 3:1–2.

21. Psalm 34:8.

22. Psalm 42:1–2.

23. Revelation 3:20.

CHAPTER 7: YOU'VE GOT TO FEED YOURSELF

1. Matthew 6:9–13. In the NIV the closing doxology is included as a textual note, but it's traditionally included in the prayer.

2. Church of the Highlands, Birmingham, Alabama, *Growth Track Book*, p. 40.

3. Robert Gelinas, *The Mercy Prayer* (Nashville: Nelson, 2013).

4. Romans 8:26–27.

5. Lamentations 3:23.

6. Psalm 92:1–2.

7. 1 Thessalonians 5:17.

8. Cf. Mark 16:12.

9. Luke 24:13–35.

10. John 20:11–18.

11. John 21:1–14.
12. Romans 10:17: "Faith comes from hearing the message, and the message is heard through the word about Christ."
13. 1 Corinthians 3:21–23: "All things are yours, whether Paul or Apollos or Cephas or the world or life or death or the present or the future—all are yours, and you are of Christ, and Christ is of God."
14. Luke 24:25.
15. James 1:22–24.
16. Romans 12:2.
17. 2 Corinthians 5:17: "If anyone is in Christ, the new creation has come: The old has gone, the new is here!"
18. 2 Timothy 3:16–17, NLT.
19. John 1:14: "The Word became flesh and made his dwelling among us."

CHAPTER 8: ARE YOU READY FOR GREATNESS?

1. Philippians 2:7.
2. Matthew 20:26–28.
3. John 13:3.
4. 1 John 4:19.
5. Acts 1:8.
6. 2 Timothy 2:2.
7. Matthew 16:18.
8. Deuteronomy 8:18.
9. Proverbs 3:9.
10. Leviticus 27:30, emphasis added.
11. Malachi 3:11: " 'I will prevent pests from devouring your crops, and the vines in your fields will not drop their fruit before it is ripe,' says the LORD."
12. Malachi 3:8–10.
13. Malachi 3:10.
14. Matthew 21:28–31.

15. Matthew 25:21.
16. Hebrews 11:6.

CHAPTER 9: FREE LIFE

1. John 8:36: "So if the Son sets you free, you will be free indeed."
2. Romans 3:23: "For all have sinned and fall short of the glory of God."
3. Romans 6:6: "For we know that our old self was crucified with him so that the body ruled by sin might be done away with, that we should no longer be slaves to sin."
4. Romans 7:25.
5. Romans 8:1−2.
6. Hebrews 12:1.
7. Hebrews 10:14: "For by one sacrifice he has made perfect forever those who are being made holy."
8. Philippians 1:6.
9. John 16:33.
10. 1 John 4:18.
11. 2 Timothy 1:7, NKJV.
12. John 15:5.
13. 1 Peter 5:7.
14. See Matthew 6:25−34.
15. Nehemiah 8:10b: "Do not grieve, for the joy of the LORD is your strength."
16. Matthew 11:28.
17. Matthew 11:29−30.
18. Philippians 4:19.
19. Jeremiah 29:11.

CHAPTER 10: FIRST THINGS FIRST

1. Genesis 1:28.
2. Philippians 2:16.
3. 2 Peter 1:3.

ACKNOWLEDGMENTS

Writing a book is like hunting; it's best done with friends. I had several with me on this journey, and it's my privilege to thank them.

First of all, my family. I couldn't have done it without the love and support of my wife, Kerri, and my kids, Kaylan, Stovie, and Annabelle.

Next up, I am grateful for the Celebration team members who contributed thoughts and feedback along the way. I couldn't have done it without Lea Sims, Linda Riddle, John Reed, and John Wyatt, and expert and insightful help in reviewing and editing the early drafts done by Lexie Goodman, Jenny Huang, and Jeff Jenkins. Joel Miller deserves special thanks for his help with some of the content and the book overall.

My agent, Esther, for believing in this project.

My editor, Carolyn; and the entire Zondervan team for your encouragement and support of the book.

And finally, my wonderful Celebration family has not only heard these ideas, but they have shown me the truth of them as we've grown together. Church, you are living proof.

ABOUT THE AUTHOR

Stovall Weems is the founder and lead pastor of Celebration Church in Jacksonville, Florida. Celebration is a growing, diverse, multisite church, with more than twelve thousand people in weekly attendance. As a pastor, teacher, writer, and sought-after conference speaker, his ministry focuses on building the local church, reaching people with the gospel, and developing passionate followers of Christ. Stovall and his wife, Kerri, have three children, Kaylan, Stovie, and Annabelle.

THE GOD FIRST LIFE NETWORK

 GODFIRSTLIFENETWORK.COM

PASTORS & LEADERS VISIT

GODFIRSTLIFENETWORK.COM FOR

INFORMATION   FREE RESOURCES

COACHING   & MORE

4/27